PUPPY TRAINING FOR BEGINNERS

THE BEGINNER'S GUIDE ON HOW TO RAISE A WELL-BEHAVED, HAPPY, AND HEALTHY DOG

MARY BUTTS

COPYRIGHT

© Copyright 2021 by Mary Butts

All rights reserved.

This document is geared towards providing exact and reliable information concerning the topic and issue covered. The publication is sold with the idea that the publisher is not required to render accounting, officially permitted or otherwise qualified services. If advice is necessary, legal or professional, a practiced individual in the profession should be ordered.

- From a Declaration of Principles which was accepted and approved equally by a Committee of the American Bar Association and a Committee of Publishers and Associations.

In no way is it legal to reproduce, duplicate, or transmit any part of this document in either electronic means or printed format. Recording of this publication is strictly prohibited, and any storage of this document is not allowed unless with written permission from the publisher. All rights reserved.

The information provided herein is stated to be truthful and consistent, in that any liability, in terms of inattention or otherwise, by any usage or abuse of any policies, processes, or directions contained within is the solitary and utter responsibility of the recipient reader. Under no circumstances will any legal responsibility or blame be held against the publisher for any reparation, damages, or monetary loss due to the information herein, either directly or indirectly.

Respective authors own all copyrights not held by the publisher.

The information herein is offered for informational purposes solely and is universal as so. The presentation of the information is without a contract or any guarantee assurance.

The trademarks that are used are without any consent, and the publication of the trademark is without permission or backing by the trademark owner. All trademarks and brands within this book are for clarifying purposes only and are owned by the owners themselves, not affiliated with this document.

CONTENTS

PUPPY TRAINING SURVIVAL GUIDE FOR HIS FIRST 30 DAYS AT HOME

POSITIVE PUPPY OFF-LEASH RECALL TRAINING

CAN'T LIVE WITHOUT YOU? 1 IN 5 DOGS ARE LIKELY TO SUFFER FROM SEPARATION ANXIETY.

INTRODUCTION

Congratulations! You have a new puppy! This will be one of the best decisions you have ever made. Your puppy will love you unconditionally, and you will love him or her just as much.

But, are you worried about caring for and training your new puppy when he or she gets home so that you can give them the perfect life? Are you worried about letting your bundle of joy off his leash? Are you concerned about potty training or leaving him alone? Or do you feel overwhelmed with how to do it all and do it fast? And what should you do if your puppy cries when you leave or makes a mess when you are not home?

Stop worrying - this book will take you through every step, and guide you through everything you need to know. It will explain how to prepare for your new puppy, how to get your puppy settled into his forever home, and then, finally, teach you how to train him walks on and off-leash.

Puppy Training For The First 30 Days has all the training you need to get him started before you are able to take him outside for walks with other dogs, on and off-leash. It covers everything from bringing him home, potty and crate training. Positive Puppy Recall covers all the final training needs including clicker, leash, and recall training (and how to greet other dogs in the park).

Can't Live Without You? helps you prevent and cure separation anxiety, one of the most common problems for today's dogs. You will discover what causes separation anxiety, how to identify separation anxiety, and how to make sure your puppy won't experience it.

In this book, I will explain the essential training that dog trainers learn and that every puppy parent needs to know. Training should involve all of the family, adults and kids alike. Everyone in your puppy's home is a parent.

This training will start as soon as your puppy is home and it will show your puppy how to live in your home and be happy and content. It will help you understand how he thinks and how to teach him using positive training. This training will help him want to do everything that you need him to do and enable your puppy to spend as much time with you as possible, everywhere and anywhere, and ensure he has the perfect life with you - even if sometimes, you are not at home.

This book includes training on:

- How to potty train and house-train your puppy
- Crate Training and the best size of crate
- Eating and examples of poisonous everyday food
- How to get your puppy to paying attention
- Indoor and enclosed recall training
- Sit, stay, and come
- Walking to heel
- Clicker training
- Leash Training
- Recall
- Using the long line
- Proofing
- Emergency stop

- Off-leash
- Going to the park
- Causes of Separation Anxiety
- How to prevent Separation Anxiety

Sometimes it feels like there is too much to learn but if you follow the training and go through each stage step-by-step, starting with Puppy Training Survival Guide For His First 30 Days At Home then you begin getting your puppy ready for recall and going outside for walks. With each step along the way, he will be learning to be happy if he is left home alone as each part of his training builds. It won't take as long as you think!

PUPPY TRAINING SURVIVAL GUIDE FOR HIS FIRST 30 DAYS AT HOME

INTRODUCTION

Congratulations on your new puppy! You might think that this little bundle of fur is the best thing you have ever done (it is) but you will also be concerned about how well you can look after him or her. There will be lots of little things you will suddenly discover you had not thought about or thought that you knew.

How often do they need to go potty? Will they like a crate and is it cruel? (no, it's not). How on earth do you teach your puppy about the house rules and will they understand what you mean? How long will all this take? How often do you need to feed them and why are they chewing everything?

All of these things are just a part of your puppy growing up, and you learning to live with them and them learning to live with you. This means both you and your puppy are both learning how to make things work.

If you can spend just a little bit of time over the first few months then you will be amazed at how fast they can learn and how much easier it is than you thought it would be.

And if you can make it all work with just this little bit of training then your puppy will grow into a happy dog that you will do so much more with than you ever imagined.

I have assumed that you have already picked your puppy and dog breed but if you haven't, I have included an overview of dog types in Chapter 7.

Finally, I don't recommend tethering your dog at home (or in the yard) or using any kind of 'punishment' collars. This includes bark collars or e-collars. I just don't believe that this type of early training can ever be good for a dog. If it is not good for your dog, it won't be good for you if you want your puppy to grow up as a valued and integrated family member.

I hope you enjoy this book. It will teach you how to potty train and house train your puppy and how to deal with the most common traits of a very young puppy who is just starting out on his journey of life. It includes the feeding and the importance of schedules as well as the mouthing phase all puppies go through. Your job, at this early stage of his development, is to help him understand how to live and how to live with you. These first few weeks that you spend with him, and before you can take him out for walks, are perhaps the most important time in you and your puppy's life. And they grow up fast. Puppies become teenagers anywhere between 4 to 8 months.

Take your time over these first weeks and months, and I promise you, you will soon forget all the mishaps along the way.

WELCOME HOME

The first thing to know about puppy training and also dog training is that you will make mistakes. And the second thing to know is that your puppy will do things that you don't expect. Each and every dog is unique, and each one will have its own ways of doing things which means that even although you have done everything right it just won't work for your puppy in the way you thought that it would. But I promise you, these unique traits will be things that you will love the most about your pup. You will look out for these things and adore them because this is what makes him your special dog.

Before you bring your puppy home

Find out what type of food your puppy has been eating up until this point. You will want to slowly introduce him to the food you want to use and you will do this by mixing some of his existing food into the new food you have for him. The reason you do this is that a sudden change in diet will upset his tummy and not only make him feel uncomfortable but can lead to unexpected accidents that the puppy just won't be in control over and make it more difficult in the first few days to start potty training successfully. You will also want to know when (and how often) your puppy is used to being fed.

To change his food, start with a small amount of his new food mixed into what he is used to, then slowly increase the amount until all of his food is the food you have chosen. This is a rule that you will follow throughout his life. Dogs don't like a sudden change to their diet, so always introduce a new dog food slowly no matter how old your dog is.

The next thing you want to try and do is have something that smells like his previous home. If the current owner or breeder doesn't have something you can take home with you, then ask if you can leave some clothing there for a week or so before you bring him home (a sock or an old towel). This will give the puppy some comfort over the first few days and be a familiar smell for him. Ideally, put this in his crate or the basket you want him to use.

Finally, if you have a garden, you will need to puppy-proof it. I can promise you, if there are any gaps in a fence or hedge, your puppy will find it and they will disappear in a second as they go exploring. Use chicken-wire or something similar. Anything will do as long as it can securely block access. I kept the chicken wire there for over a year and removed it bit-by-bit, checking to see if the young dog (he's called Barney) noticed the area beyond the garden that could be just within reach. (I still watch him, even now, and he is already 5 years old!). Millie, the older dog, was never too bothered by what might be next door but Barney was always curious as a puppy.

You will also want to puppy-proof your house. Make sure there are no wires that he can easily chew and that there is nothing he can reach that you don't want him to. Puppies are extremely curious.

Don't forget to check what house plants you have. Some of them can be toxic to dogs. These include lilies, aloe vera, ivy and cyclamen. It's better to keep all houseplants out of the way of your puppy and double check to make sure yours aren't a threat to him.

And don't forget to pick the name of your puppy! You will want to know this as soon as he gets home so you can start training him by using it.

Remember, mixing in some games with the potty and crate training is a great way to get the kids, and everyone else, involved in the care of your new puppy. This means before your puppy arrives, think about who can do what and try and get the family or other household members involved as early as you can (this is also good for helping to prevent separation anxiety).

He's arrived!

When your pup comes home you will already ideally want to have his crate or basket ready. You will have the same type of dog food that he was being fed and you will have the item placed in his crate or basket that smells like his previous home.

Over the first few nights, he is likely to miss his old family. It is okay over these first nights to take his crate or basket into your room but, ideally, only do this for the first few nights. He also won't be used to lots of noise and activity around him. Try and keep things as calm as you can and make sure to create some 'time-outs' for him.

You can introduce him to his crate by placing it in the room with you.

Don't forget that puppies sleep a lot. They also need their sleep so try and let them have their sleep time even although everyone is going to want to play with your new puppy and pick them up and cuddle them. This is okay and it is actually great for the puppy to have lots of affection and integrate into the entire life of his new family, so just be aware of it.

In terms of picking them up and cuddling them, try not to overdo their handling especially if they have not been used to it. Constantly picking them up will be something their little bodies are not used to and, just like us, if we get picked up too much then it can become uncomfortable and even sore. This isn't anything to worry too much about but it's handy to be aware of how often they are being handled.

And, of course, being picked up by different people gets them used to other people from an early age.

The best way to pick up your puppy is to put your hands between his front legs and around his chest. Then pull him towards your chest and, at about the same time, and when he is safely secured, take one of your hands and use it to support his bottom so that you are supporting his weight. Don't forget to take a sniff of his breath! A puppy's breath is a unique smell so grab your chance while you can! It disappears quickly and I would not recommend doing this later, when the smell may not be quite so sweet!

As mentioned earlier, puppies sleep a lot. They will easily sleep for 7-8 hours at night and they will generally sleep up to 14 hours a day. I will talk about a schedule later and it will include sleep time for him.

Socialization

In its simplest form socialization is how you and your puppy learn to communicate with each other and how your puppy learns about others that he lives with and meets. This includes other humans and other dogs.

In your puppy's first few weeks in his new home, this is crucial training. In the first week or two, this is difficult because your puppy will to yet be vaccinated but you can still carry him, take him out in your car, and have others come to the house to meet him.

This is also the best time to touch their ears, mouth, tails, and paws and to get him used to you doing this. This part of training is often missed but it will really help later with grooming or if you need to inspect him for any injury. Sit with him quietly so that you are also teaching him how to relax with you and touch his ears or mouth and give him a treat and reward him when he remains calm and relaxed.

If you can, take your puppy to any socialization classes, where they can meet other young puppies and their parents. They will play around for 20 or 30 minutes but they learn how to communicate with other dogs and how 'far they can go'. They also learn about meeting other humans who are not the family.

Vaccinations over the first year

It's a good idea to talk to your vet about your puppy's vaccination requirements as soon as you can. Below is a summary of the recommended vaccinations from the American Kennel Club and there are also optional vaccinations that you can give your puppy. I have only highlighted the recommended vaccinations here.

6-8 weeks - Distemper, parvovirus

10-12 weeks - DHPP (for distemper, adenovirus (hepatitis), parainfluenza, parvovirus

16-18 weeks DHPP, rabies

12-16 months DHPP, rabies

Unvaccinated puppies less than 4 months old are most at risk of Parvovirus. Parvovirus is contagious and affects all dogs. There is no cure and the puppy will need to be kept hydrated and an effort made to control the secondary symptoms.

The Kennel Club recommends talking to your veterinarian about Heartworm treatment when your puppy is 12-16 weeks old. This is a preventative medication that is taken regularly.

These are the sort of issues where any recommendation must come from a qualified pet health professional who understands the laws and problems in your area and who will be aware of any breed-specific problems. Make sure that you ask your veterinarian for advice.

Your puppy can go outside for a walk in the park after his third set of vaccinations (around weeks 16-18). It is also at this point that he can exercise forum to 20 minutes at a time. He can also now meet unfamiliar dogs. Before this, you can take them to your yard around 7 days after his first set of vaccinations but avoid other dogs. Your yard must be enclosed to ensure no other dogs have been there. His feet must also not touch the ground in public spaces. If you live in an apartment you might need to do this during potty training and to let your puppy potty, Pick one spot and carry him there and back but you can let him sniff around that spot.

After his second vaccination, you can take him for a walk on paved surfaces but not on grass or places where you can't see if other dogs have urinated or gone to the toilet although I would also suggest that you carry him rather than walk on any surface. It is still important for them not to meet unfamiliar dogs. It is at this stage, when he is just under 18 weeks, that you can take him to his puppy socialization classes at the local pet store or your vet (where all the other puppies will be at the same vaccination stage).

HOUSE AND POTTY TRAINING

One of the main reasons people don't want to have a puppy is the thought of potty training, or specifically, the thought of a dog that is not house-trained.

House training or potty training your puppy will be one of the first things you do when your puppy comes home. It can be done, so don't worry, but there will be a few accidents along the way. And that's okay too. It won't last for long and the benefits of having your pup with you for the years that follow are well worth the odd mishap or two. In fact, you will forget that you had to house-train and even how you did it.

The speed at which your pup learns will vary and can also depend on where they came from or if any training has already started in their previous homes. I know this sounds obvious, especially ion you have an adopted puppy, but even a young puppy's rate of being house trained will depend on what they were being taught once they were being weaned and walking confidently on their 4 legs.

When we had a litter of 7 spaniels, and we started to train the puppies to go to the puppy pad we had on the floor as soon as they reached the stage of being able to move around and were occasionally getting to venture outside. We used puppy pads and we started by moving the pads closer to the door, and eventually outside. This meant when they went to their forever-homes they were easy to train and complete the house training.

How long can a puppy wait for the toilet

Don't forget that a puppy's bladder also grows with them. When they are younger it is smaller and this means that they will need to empty it more often.

Generally speaking, a puppy's ability to hold its bladder increases by about an hour per month.

This will mean that at one month they can hold on for about an hour. By 2 months old, they should be able to hold on for about 2 hours before they need to relieve themselves.

Try not to make them hold on for much more than this over the first few months or there will be accidents and try to make sure that your time away from them can tie into their need to go toilet.

As a general rule, puppies under 6 months will struggle to hold their bladder for more than 3 or 4 hours and this should help you work out how long you can be away or when you might need to try and get someone to visit your puppy so that they can relieve themselves outside, rather than in their crate, or in the room they are in.

In terms of pooping, a puppy will poop after food. If you feed your puppy before you leave, make sure that you feed them around 45 minutes before you are due to leave. This gives you time to take them for a poop. They will normally need to poop between 5 and 30 minutes after a meal. Millie used to poop about 5 minutes after her meal while Barney was about 20 minutes.

If you are playing with your puppy before you leave, then take them out for a poop after the playtime as this can also make them want to poop.

Puppy Pads

In terms of starting the potty training, the best thing I have done is used puppy pads.

On the same theme of puppy pads, the very best thing I ever tried was a puppy pad that looked like grass. For some reason, it really worked. I used it with the seven puppies before they left for their forever homes and they all used it.

Whether you use a fabric pad or a fake grass one, these are the things you need to do.

I started by placing the puppy pad in the room as soon as my puppy, Millie, came home. When she looked like she was about to potty I would place her on the pad and if she relieved herself she got lots of praise. It didn't take much time at all before they would go to the pad, probably around 2 days.

I then started to move the puppy pad towards the door I wanted her to use to go out. Try not to move it too far from where you started the training, just move it slowly to the door. Once at the door I let her get used to that for a day or two then I moved the pad just outside the door. In the final stages, if I saw her starting to pee or potty, I would gently pick her up and place her on the pad, and then I would take her and the pad outside. If there wasn't enough time to do this I would just place her on the pad.

You might want to consider placing the puppy pad at the door he will be using to access his outside area right away. This will depend on how far the room the household congregates is from that door.

At every point give your puppy lots of praise.

This process can take more time than it might need to. As long as you remember that he will want to relieve himself when he wakes up, after play, or after he eats then you have a head-start in terms of knowing when to expect activity.

It's important to never punish or get angry with your puppy if he toilets in the house. You sometimes see a recommendation to push their face into the mess. Don't do this. It will do the opposite of helping. They won't understand and will be scared. Getting angry or pushing them may only mean that they don't want to potty in front of you and learn to avoid it.

How to manage their potty training

Puppy's being puppies (and later dogs) love praise and rewards.

Once your puppy begins the process of going outside to potty, don't forget that every time he relieves himself outdoors, you need to praise him and give him a treat. But don't do this while he is in the action of potty-time - he will stop to seek the reward, get distracted, and won't finish what he started which means that he won't be fully relieved when he goes back inside. Wait until he has finished and do this every single time he goes outdoors for their potty.

As you do this, use a phrase that he will start to recognize (try not to use 'Good boy' or 'Good girl' - it might cause confusion!). I used to say 'Be a good girl' and, on reflection, this wasn't a great idea. Use a short phrase such as 'potty' or 'poo poo' or whatever you feel comfortable saying and will remember - just make sure it is one that your pup can begin to recognize with the action he is being asked to complete. This is a key step because they need to know exactly what behavior the reward is for.

This is not only useful when your puppy is young. Millie, my older dog, had soft tissue damage to her knee on her hind leg. This meant that she struggled to walk and had difficulty 'sitting down' to toilet. When I carried her to the garden to try and get her to 'do pee-pee', this was much easier because I could say a phrase and she knew exactly what I wanted her to do. Although she tried her best to 'poo-poo' she didn't manage this for over a day but I was greatly relieved when she finally 'pee-peed'. Because I could ask her what to do, she knew what to try to do. It's good to remember that much of what you teach now will be of great help throughout your puppy's life. It's also good to think about what phrase you are going to be stuck with for a long time!

Where?

Choose a place or a small area outside that you are him to relieve himself. As he relieves himself say your word or a specific phrase. Always take him to the same place every time you take him out to potty - in the morning, the last thing at night, after food or play during the day. If you are using training pads overnight, take the soiled pad to the area where you want your puppy toilet. The scent can help him.

When it is time to take him outside to toilet, avoid playing with your puppy and getting him excited before he toilets. Remember, they are easily distracted and will forget what they are there to do.

If your puppy looks a bit confused or doesn't toilet right away just try to encourage him to sniff the ground beside the area you want him to use. Stay outside with him until he has toileted. If nothing happens after 5 minutes take him back inside but watch him closely. After 10 minutes take him out again and keep repeating the process until they have done what you need them to do.

The signs to watch out for

Try and supervise your puppy all of the time when you are trying to potty train him. I know this is very hard to do as they tend to have a mind and vision of their own. A funny tip, not related but really ought to be, is to hide the toilet paper. They don't intend to use it for the purpose intended! They really do run away with it. The seven puppies we had found the bathroom and dragged the toilet roll through the house. I still don't know how they knew to go there nor did I realize how fast they could move.

But, by supervising and watching them, you will notice not only how they look when they start to feel uncomfortable because they need to toilet, but you will notice how they do it. They might start circling or sniffing the floor, they might be restless and may try and go to a place they have previously done their business.

If you see your puppy mid-toilet then pick him up and take him outside and try to get him to finish what he started there. If he does then gently praise him.

Now, this is hard to describe and I don't think I have ever seen it actually written down, but watch your puppy's bottom. When they need to go poop you will notice their rear end swelling outwards. This means a poop is imminent. To this day I watch Millie and Barney's rear ends when we are out walking (usually it's the start of a walk) and I get the poop bags ready. Millie always goes at the start of the walk or at the end. Barney is often too excited to play at the start but mid-walk, he starts to seek out clumps of grass or trees. He prefers something to poop 'on'.

As you will learn, or already know, puppies and dogs, are all a bit different in how they prefer to poop and pee.

When Millie was a puppy, she was obviously getting restless and looking around for a place to pee-pee. In terms of poops, she is less discerning. She still behaves like this today. Barney will pee anywhere, but he is very careful about where he poops.

Barney, when he was a puppy, just looked a 'certain way' and eventually started moving towards the door but he never actually 'asked' out. He still does this - he never asks out vocally. He just stands beside the door without a noise whereas Millie whines. When Barney was young, he was really difficult to read because he didn't do any of the obvious things like scratching at the door, sniffing, or circling. When he was younger, the poops always came as surprise to him. He would go for a pee and suddenly discover a poop was coming. He was always surprised by this. I still don't really understand why but there will be something I did not do as best as I could at some point and I am researching this. He is fine now but he likes to poop on top of clumps of grass or bushes rather than in an open field.

He now has a short sharp bark if he is really desperate and I haven't already noticed him patiently standing beside the door, but that's it. He will quietly wait silently for as long as he can and then give his bark.

Watch out for any of those signs or watch out for something your dog does that might signal a change in behavior in how they are feeling. Watch their bottoms as sometimes, like Barney, they don't even know what's coming. This is the part where they train us. We need to watch and learn what they are telling us. As soon as you notice any of these things then take them outside. If they relieve themselves then follow up with your praise and treats.

Some trainers would advise that the dog is tethered in the home on a long leash - around 6 feet. I don't think this needs to be the case. I am not even sure I think that it should ever be done or recommended. It simply just can't be a good way to train your puppy nor to teach them about their home. I have never tethered any dog in the house. I would though recommend keeping them to just one or two rooms as you go through the house-training process - and be vigilant and watch and learn and stay with them if you can but don't tether them.

Leaving the house and overnight

Your puppy won't be able to hold his bladder all night long for severe months. This means it is likely that he will need to go during the night. Put some newspaper or puppy pads in his crate but try and place them in an area that he can avoid. In the morning, don't forget to take the soiled pad or newspaper to his garden area. If you are going out for any length of time then do the same thing but try, if you can, to be no more than 3 hours at the start.

It may take several months before your puppy is fully house trained but the accidents will become less frequent. Try and be patient. It will pay off in time and in just a few short years you will have forgotten all about your trials and tribulations of potty training your puppy.

How to clean up the mess

It's important to clean the area and try to remove the scent. Don't use ammonia-based products as this will just encourage them to go to the same place again. You can use biological power and some people swear by a vinegar-water mix. I have tried this but I am not convinced it works although I do know other dog owners where this has worked wonders,

Create a Schedule

One of the best and most effective, ways to train your puppy is to get him used to a schedule. The schedule will also help you too.

The key aspects of your schedule will be feeding times, sleeping time (puppies like to sleep a lot), and of course, potty time.

Your schedule

When you first bring your puppy home make sure that you take them out frequently.

Take them out as soon as they wake up, after playing and after they have eaten or had a drink.

A useful summary of what you need to do is detailed in these 5 steps

- Feed them at the same time
- Feed them with the same frequency, for example, every 2 hours depending on their age
- Take them out them out as soon as they wake up
- Take them out before they go to bed
- Take them out after food and after play.

In terms of how a day might look, try not to forget his sleep time, Your puppy will get sleepy after eating. Just make sure that you take him out to potty right after he has eaten but before he goes for his first morning nap. I tend to let my dogs out as soon as they wake up, I then feed them breakfast and play with them for 20-30 minutes (depending on how much time I have), then I take them out again before they fall asleep. They have been doing this schedule since they were young pups and they seem to like it. These days, as adults, they potty either when they wake up or after breakfast.

Sleep

As mentioned earlier, puppies sleep a lot. When he is young, and up to 3 months old, he can sleep18 hours a day, and sometimes up to 20! He can fall asleep suddenly, and it can even appear as if he has fallen asleep mid-step. He will fall asleep with a chew in their mouth or just sit down in the middle of the floor and collapse. When he does, just pick him up and put him in his cage or basket (with the door open).

He should easily sleep for 7 hours at night and most puppies can sleep for 7 hours without requiring a bathroom break.

Puppies need their sleep so make sure you don't forget to let him get it. This will be harder than you think in the first few weeks. There will be lots of visitors and lots of people who will want to pick him up and give him a cuddle. This is okay but don't forget to give him his sleep-time. He needs it.

Time	Activity
7:00 AM	Wake up and go outside
7:30 AM	Breakfast
7:45 AM	Playtime
8:00 AM	Outside for toilet
8:15 AM	Seep (with toy in the cage/depart for work?)
10:15 AM	Outside for toilet
10:30 AM	Food
10:40 AM	Outside for toilet
10:50 AM	Playtime
11:10 AM	Outside for toilet
11:15 AM	Sleep with Kong or Toy in the cage
1:15 PM	Wake up/ outside for toilet
1:20 PM	Food
1:25 PM	Outside for toilet/playtime
1:30 PM	Playtime
2:00 PM	Outside for toilet
2:15 PM	Sleep (cage with toy)

Build this into your schedule so that it might look like this:

And so on. You will find a schedule that works for you as you discover when your pup likes to go potty during the day. It might be after food or after playtime. But always take him out as soon as he wakens.

At the end of the day, it will be outside for the toilet, then to his cage or basket.

These timings will change as he gets a bit older and sleeps less - but he will always sleep a great deal and for at least 14 hours a day.

Bedtime

You will find that your puppy will start to go to bed by himself. He will get used to your schedule and will fit into when you go to bed at night.

In the early days, if they do wake up during the night, don't make a fuss and do not be tempted to play with them. They will be more than happy to play but they need to know that this is not the right time.

Don't turn on all the lights either. Keep things like 'night time'. Take them outside to let them toilet and then return them to bed.

Dogs should always have access to water. However, at night, and about one to two hours before he goes to bed, remove his water bowl (make sure he has had a recent drink first, he needs his water).

CRATE TRAINING

Many people worry that using a crate might be cruel. If used properly, a crate is a place that your puppy will feel safe and happy. This is the main objective of your crate training. It brings a range of other benefits that will mean your life with your puppy can be as full and engaging as possible - and allow him to be included in almost all of your activities and even holidays. The most important use of a crate is to provide a safe place for your puppy. Never use the crate as punishment or as a 'sin bin'.

Crate training is often one of the main used alongside housetraining to help speed up both of the processes.

The reason using the crate works for potty training is that dogs don't like to mess where they sleep and where they relax. The puppy will not mess here especially if you have crate trained so that they see their crate as their safe place or their den. What's more, if they are sleeping in their crate they will do their very best to hold on until they can leave the crate.

This puts you in more control because you will know where the puppy is and what he might want to do when you open the door or when he leaves his create. This means as soon as your puppy leaves his crate (or you let him out), take him outside. He will soon get used to this routine, especially when he gets his praise and reward.

Crate training has lots of other benefits. Your dog will be able to travel with you more easily, in the car or on a plane. You will be able to visit friends and family more easily because you can you the crate as their portable den. You can go out knowing that you won't return to chewed furniture or a general mess (the chewing usually only occurs with puppies) and your dog can use the create as his bed and sleep there overnight.

In summary, the create gives your dog and puppy somewhere safe to rest and to sleep. It helps them feel comfortable when you leave the house or they are in a new house and it means that your dog can enjoy more of your life outside of the home if you need to travel. It also helps them settle into a dog sitter they need to stay with a sitter when you go on vacation.

Introducing your pup to the crate

After you have picked your crate and before the puppy arrives, add a blanket or something soft for your puppy to lie on. If you are using a second-hand crate, make sure you wash it thoroughly to remove any scent of the previous dog who may have been using it.

If you are using a wire crate have something close that you can place on the top or on the side of the crate. This can help with making it feel more like a den especially at night. Don't cover up all four sides and make sure the front of the crate with the door is left uncovered.

Place the crate in a room that is used by the rest of the household. This will help the puppy get used to the crate without being separate from you and from your puppy's new family and it will mean he doesn't feel alone and scared. A puppy will not be used to being alone and it will make him anxious and scared especially when he first arrives at his new home.

When your puppy comes home, place his toys and the item that came from his previous early home into the crate.

The first stage is to place some food around the crate. If he doesn't start moving towards the crate or being curious about it all by themselves, then entice him by calling him to the crate in a happy tone of voice and by throwing tasty treats around, and near, the crate. keep trying until he starts to come over to the crate and begins to feel comfortable around it.

The next stage is to slowly start moving the treats to the door and then inside the crate. Give him lots of praise at all stages. Only start moving the food inside the crate once he has started getting used to the outside of the crate. As he starts to enter the crate, don't close the door.

Keep playing the game and move the treats or food deeper into the crate. Just let him enter and leave and explore if he wants to. You want to get him used to entering and leaving by himself.

This can take anything from 10 minutes to a few days, depending on his experience to date, to get him to go into his crate by himself. Keep the training sessions to between 3 and 5 minutes.

If for any reason your puppy is not responding to food and treats then entice him with his favorite toy.

The next phase is to increase the length of time he spends in his crate. You can do this by feeding him in his crate or you can put a Kong toy filled with treats into the cage for him to play with.

If he is reluctant to go into the crate then put his food bowl beside the crate door and then slowly move it into the crate until he will eat at the back of the crate.

Once he is happy entering and leaving and maybe lingering for a few minutes in his crate then try to close the door. You can try to do this when he is eating food but one of the most effective ways is to give him his Kong stuffed with something he loves. Wait until he starts to become engrossed in getting his food out then slowly close the door. If you close the door and he gets anxious or scared immediately open the door.

If he does nothing then wait for a few minutes before opening the door again.

Keep increasing the length of time before you open the door - you want to try and reach 10 minutes. If he shows any signs of distress, if he is panting, whining, cowering, or showing any signs of aggression, then you will know you have increased the time too quickly.

Once your puppy is happy to stay in the crate up to 10 minutes after eating or playing then you will know that he is now likely to understand that his crate is a safe space.

The next phase of his crate training can now begin and this is when you move out of sight while he is in his crate with the door closed.

This is the stage when his toys and his Kong (filled with food, peanut butter, or soft cheese) will really help. Put his toys in his cage and close the door once he has entered. Stay beside the crate for around 5 minutes before moving quietly from the room and out of sight. Once you are out of sight turn around and come back to the side of the crate and sit beside it for 5 minutes. Gradually start to stay out of sight longer. Do this throughout the day but at different times. You will need to repeat the process several times. If you hear any barking or whining do not come back mid bark or mid whine. Try and find a gap and this is when you return. You are aiming to increase the time you are out of sight to around 30 minutes.

Once this has been achieved you can start leaving the house altogether. But remember to provide toys for him to play with so that he does not get bored. Before leaving make sure he has had a small meal, had been exercised, and remember to leave calmly without any fuss.

In terms of sleeping at night, in the early days, you can put the crate in your bedroom at night. `You only want to do this for a few days - not any longer. When your puppy first arrives home, he will have been used to sleeping with other puppies so letting him sleep in his crate in your room will help him settle in.

Once you put the crate into the room where he will spend his time at night, make sure to turn out the lights when you (and he) go to bed. You can leave a low-level one on if you like but make sure it isn't bright.

This will also mean that if you do need to take them out during the night, they will recognize that this is sleep time. And don't forget, that if you do need to take them out during the night, don't turn on all the lights.

Size and Types of Crate

There are 3 main types of crate. A plastic crate (or box) a wire crate or cage and one made of fabric - I think of this as a travel carry case that can be used both as a safe place and for travel.

Most of my experience is with a cage and a fabric crate but I know many people who use a plastic crate. This choice really is up to you.

What size?

Unlike the material that the crate is made from, and as you would expect, the size of the crate you choose is important.

If the crate is too small it will make your dog uncomfortable and it is too big it can make your dog insecure. You need to know both the height, width, and length of the crate (or kennel).

The easiest thing to do is to try and get an idea of how big your puppy might grow. If you are training an older dog (or a dog over 12 months old) then measure from the top of his nose to the base of his tail. It's also a good idea to measure the height of your dog when he is sitting down. To estimate the crate size, you will need to add around 2 to 4 inches to your measurement for heights and 1 to 2 inches for the length. The width is less important as it will relate to the height. A list of dog breed sizing and the dogs that broadly fall into each grouping, including height and weight, are detailed in Chapter 7.

The next thing you need to do is check the weight of your dog or, in terms of your puppy, check the average weight of his breed when fully grown. Then make sure and check the weight limits on the crate that you are buying (or you may be able to pick it up from another dog owner who is no longer using their crate). To save you from buying different crates as your puppy grows, you can section off a part of the crate with a separator to make it smaller when he is smaller.

FOOD AND FEEDING

As you might expect, feeding and pooping are closely related!

You need to get your puppy into a regular schedule. The quicker you can do this, and get him used to this schedule, then the easier everything becomes. Creating a schedule really can make a big difference.

Feeding them to the same schedule also means that they will want to relieve themselves in reaction to that schedule. This, in itself, will make it easier for you to house-train.

What to feed them

Dogs are built to be meat eaters but they are descended from omnivores so they can survive adequately without meat (if the protein balance is right). The protein in meat is not the same as the protein found in plant-based foods and this is one of the reasons to be careful of the food you give your puppy and your dog. This doesn't mean that dogs can't live on a plant-based diet, it just means it will need to be supplement with the essential proteins he will require and Vitamin D.

Balancing nutrition is the most important aspect of your dogs' food.

For example, we need our carbs for energy but dogs don't need a lot of carbs.

Dogs and especially puppies need fats and fatty acids. Most of these are contained in animal fats but some seed and plant oils can provide a concentrated source of energy. You are looking for an Omega-3 family of essential fatty acids.

When you are looking for dog food, therefore, look at the type of calories rather than the overall total. You don't want too much carbohydrate. The average dog food today can contain anywhere between 30% and 70% carbohydrates but in the wild dogs will intake only about 15%. An adult dog's diet can contain up to 50% of carbohydrate (by weight), up to 4.5% fiber, and a minimum of around 5.5% should come from fats, and 10% from protein. You can read more about nutrition at nap.edu and this is listed in the resources at the end of this book.

In general, though, if you want to check out how much meat is in your dog food take a look at the ingredients list. The further down the meat appears, the lower to content. The most common ingredients today are whole grain, fat, soya, and corn. If you see chicken by-products this doesn't mean it is chicken meat. It most likely isn't.

The top ingredients to look for (and look for a range of these in the same food) include deboned chicken or turkey, Atlantic mackerel and herring, chidden and turkey liver, chicken and turkey heart, and other items such as egg and other types of fish. All high in protein.

There has also been some debate about dry food versus wet food. The main difference is that wet food contains more water (around 75%) whereas dry food can contain only about 10% water. Dry food tends to be more calorie-dense and wet food has less grain and fewer carbs. Grain isn't necessarily a bad thing, it just depends on quantity.

Dry food lasts for longer and tends to be more cost-effective than wet food.

There are lots of choices on the market and you will want to research this yourself. I feed Millie and Barney wheat-free dry fish-based kibble but I do try and change this from time to time. I have now found a brand that they love. It comes from a local farm producer. Sometimes, I mix in some wet food. They really love this and I quite like the mix of wet and dry food as a balance. It's also important to try and add some things in now-and-again to give your dog a little change.

How much to feed

Puppies can require up to double the energy intake of adult dogs. This is based on weight - it doesn't mean they eat twice as much as they do as an adult just that per pound of weight they do - and they weigh a lot less when they are puppies. Small breeds of dogs can reach their adult weight in nine to twelve months. Medium, large and giant-breed puppies can eat too much at this stage and this might lead to bone or joint problems later. This means it is best to control their feeding and not leave food in their bowl for them to nibble on between meals.

The frequency really does depend on how old they are. A puppy's tummy is small when he arrives home and will grow over time. The means you need to feed smaller amounts more regularly. Puppies aged 8-16 weeks need to be fed 4 meals a day, perhaps every 3 hours. Pups ages 3 to 6 months should be fed 3 times a day (every 4 hours) and then after that twice a day, in the morning and early evening. You are aiming to try and spread their nutrition throughout the day so space out the times to equal intervals across the day. But remember not to feed your puppy just before or after their walk (or playtime).

The amount that you feed your puppy will depend on their weight and age. The dog food you choose will also have a variety of different protein levels. When you decide on your dog food the packaging will tell you how much to feed your puppy depending on their weight. If you are in any doubt, ask your veterinary.

What not to feed - dangerous foods for your dog

Alcohol - under no circumstances give your dog alcohol. In the worst-case scenario, alcohol can cause death.

Caffeine and Chocolate - Don't give your puppy anything with caffeine. Things that can include caffeine are obviously coffee, but chocolate can also contain caffeine. Chocolate, especially dark chocolate, should never be given to your dog. The toxic substances can cause vomiting, irregular heart function, and even death. If your dog has eaten a lot of chocolate contact your veterinarian and immediately try to encourage your dog to vomit.

Onion, Chives, and Garlic - these can cause irritation in the bowel and are toxic to dogs.

Nuts (Pecans, Almonds, Walnuts, Macadamia) - these have the potential to not only cause vomiting but possible pancreatitis. Peanuts and popcorn are okay.

Raisins and grapes - avoid giving your dog raisins or grapes. The effect the toxins have is still not definitive but it can cause Kidney failure.

Coconut (including coconut oil) - in small quantities this might cause stomach upsets but coconut water should not be given to your dog.

Turkey and chicken bones. Generally speaking, be careful of any bones that you give your dog to chew. If they can easily break them apart, they can lodge in their throats or in their intestines. Even lamb joint bones can be dangerous for dogs that can chew through them and they can be quite brittle. Sharp bones can also puncture their digestive tract.

Shellfish - some dogs are ok with shellfish but one of my dogs will vomit immediately and this will happen with even small traces of shellfish such as prawns or langoustine. This doesn't mean dogs can't eat fish. They can eat fish and fish is good for them in many cases. Always ensure it is cooked and sufficiently cooled.

CHEWING AND MOUTHING

Mouthing

Puppies not only chew but there is a period when they will use their mouths - a lot! This is called mouthing and their tiny teeth are remarkably sharp.

They will grab your trouser legs or put their mouth around your hands - and their sharp teeth will take your breath away.

Puppies need to learn about different textures - and human skin is just one of the textures they need to learn about. They also need to understand how hard they can close their mouths and when enough is enough. They can only learn this by doing it. If you have children by very aware of this.

All puppies will go through this phase and you will want to teach them what some people call bite inhibition. This is something that puppies, who have come from a larger litter, will have learned a bit about because they usually learn this through play with other puppies (and something early socialization classes can help with too). There were many times when Millie had her brood of seven puppies that we heard squeals of outrage or pain as they pushed each other over and mouthed at ears, paws, and anything they could get their mouths around. When one of the pups squealed, they would stop playing, but so did the protagonist. That pup tended to look as surprised as the pup that got a sharp tooth implanted into it. Yet, just a few moments later, they were back playing. It was notable that the pup that got the painful nip was pretty eager to try this out on one of the other unsuspecting puppies.

This is just a part of a puppy growing up and learning boundaries. But it doesn't make is easier or any less painful. However, over time, all seven seemed to understand each other and know how hard a bite they could get away with. The screams of surprise between them became less frequent.

Puppies are most likely to try and mouth you when you are playing with them or tickling their tummy or petting them.

I decided to copy the pups and later discovered that this is a common training method.

It's important to let your puppy mouth you. Let him have your hand. When he closes his mouth too hard and his sharp teeth become painful squeals like a puppy or use the word "stop" and stop playing. Just let your hand go limp so that is no fun to play with. This should stop your puppy for a moment or two. He will be just as surprised as you. When he relaxes his mouth and stops then praise him. Then let him have your hand again. He will definitely go too far many times, so just keep repeating over a 15- or 20-minute time interval until he learns how hard he can close his mouth without hurting you. If your squealing and "stop' doesn't work then put him on the "naughty step' so to speak. Stop playing with him for 30 seconds or so. After this, start playing with again. If he does it again then repeat and if this still doesn't work then move away from him as soon as he mouths you and you feel that nip.

As the hard biting stops, you will want to continue teaching him as he moves his mouthing levels down from sore to moderate. Slowly teach him not to mouth at all. Eventually, he will know exactly the level of pressure that he can safely apply when he is playing.

Remember not to jerk your hands away from your puppy when he starts mouthing you. He still thinks this is a game and is more likely to lunge forward. Don't wave your hands in front of his face for the same reason - he will think it's a game.

Whatever you do, don't hit your puppy for mouthing. This will only make him play harder and it may also cause him to fear you.

Once you have done this you really want him to learn not to mouth at all on human skin and to let you pet them without being mouthed. When you puppy tries to mouth you when you are petting them, distract him by giving him a treat or a chew toy. I ended up using a tug toy with Millie. I waved it in front of her and just said "Play Tug".

This worked really well because she would follow me around trying to grab my ankles to play with me. I just stopped and said "play tug". When she stopped trying to grab my ankles, I would praise her. Eventually, I could walk around without being tailed by a puppy with sharp teeth.

One last thing to bear in mind. Like all toddlers, puppies can have tantrums. His body will be stiffer, and his mouth might be tighter around the lips. If you notice this while you are playing with him just stop the play. Don't squeal if he bites you (it will be harder than normal). If you are holding him, stop playing but continue to hold him for a few seconds then let him go. Don't make him afraid of you - you just want him to know that he has gone too far. If you notice that your puppy continues to have tantrums then you will need to get more help from a professional.

Chewing

All puppies enjoy and need to chew. They do this not only to explore their environment and to understand the texture of things but simply because they don't have hands and they like to pick things up. The only way he can explore is to use his mouth.

Between the ages of around three and seven months, your puppy will also start to experience discomfort in his mouth as the teething process gets underway. He will chew to help removed his baby teeth and he will chew to help with the pain of his adult teeth erupting in his gums.

As your puppy starts to reach adolescence, around seven to 12 months, his chewing is going to get worse. There are two possible reasons for this. It is around now that they tend to get easily bored so try to find new games (especially mental exercise games) and other games to keep them occupied. It is also around this time that their adult teeth are settling into the jaw and this can be uncomfortable for some dogs.

Your puppy is going to chew at things. In my case it was furniture. The legs of tables and the sides of the sofa and your shoes. You need to teach all of the household to put their shoes out of reach and preferably out of sight. Puppies love shoes - they are just about the right consistency of hard and soft. Perfect for exploring different textures. Much the same as furniture.

Don't forget that your puppy will chew all his life, although never quite as bad as he did in his first year. He will continue to chew because it relaxes him and he simply enjoys it. It is also a calming activity.

All dogs like to chew and some breeds are more likely to chew than others. For example, Labradors and Staffordshire Bull Terriers tend to have a stronger desire to chew.

Here are some chew toys and tips that might help.

Try and change your dog's chew toys regularly by rotating them every few days. This will prevent him from getting bored and start looking for something else to chew that might look more interesting.

Try and remove anything that you don't want him to chew and keep them well out of reach. I lost a TV remote control and a pair of glasses by forgetting to move them to higher ground. Don't forget to remove anything that might be dangerous to your puppy when he cannot be supervised.

If you find your puppy chewing on something that is not allowed, don't punish him or shout at him. This will only make him anxious. Simply distract his attention and then direct him to a chew that you want him to play with. When he starts to play with it, make a fuss of him.

Types of Chew

Many hard plastic toys are not made for chewing by a dog. The best chew toys are made of the type of hard rubber that you get with your Kong. You can also consider activity balls (and like Kong's you can place kibble, cheese spread, peanut butter, or other treat or food inside). Ropes are also good but avoid nylon or anything that the dog can pull apart into a string.

Chews such as dental chews or other edible chews can distract your puppy - they can be eaten quite quickly. These chews last just a few minutes with Barney so I tend to use them less as a chew alternative. Some dogs can chew for quite some time on these though. This is just a case of testing which chews your puppy likes the most.

BASIC COMMANDS

In the first few weeks that your puppy is home, there is some basic training that you can start right away that can teach him some of the basic commands that you will use throughout his life.

Always keep the training sessions to between 5 and 10 minutes. If he comes up against something he can't do then return to something that he can do so that you can praise and reward him at the end of the training session.

Getting to know his name

Always reward your puppy when he responds to his name. It doesn't matter how or why he is responding to his name, it only matters that he is and that you need to reward him for doing so. This might be harder to do when he is chewing something that he shouldn't be.

Don't ever be tempted to use his name as punishment. He won't understand and will be confused by your use of his name and confused by your behavior and annoyance.

Teach him to 'come'

Sit with your puppy and say his name and then the command 'come'.

Or just use the command 'come'. Each time you say the word give him a treat. If you are sitting with him, he probably won't need to 'come' but you are just teaching him that reward comes with that word.

The place a treat near you and let him eat the treat. As soon as he is finished say his name and when acknowledges his name give him another treat.

Start throwing the treat a bit further away and repeat. As soon as he turns his head towards you when you call give him praise and give him a treat.

Finally, throw it even further, call his name then let take a few steps back and let him chase you (he will love the chase game). When he reaches you, give him lots of praise and a treat. He will love this game and he will love coming back to you. Coming back is fun!

Teach him to Sit

There are a few ways to teach your puppy to sit but I have used this one to the best effect.

Sit down beside your puppy holding a treat then put the treat in front of his nose, slowly lifting it up above his head. As he tilts his head to follow the treat, he is likely to sit as he tries to reach the treat. I would usually say the word 'sit' just before his bottom touches the ground. Then, as soon as his bottom touches the ground reward him with the treat. Your puppy is learning the word sit but also starting to recognize your hand, signal. Keep doing this, eventually removing the treat from your hand but using your hand to get him to sit and saying the word sit as you start to raise your hand to the single position.

The other way to teach them to sit seems to be something that kids are really good at teaching.

Just stand in front of your puppy with his treats and ask him to sit. Then wait for him to sit and as soon as he does, reward him with praise and a treat. Move away from your position so that he needs to stand up then repeat. After a few successful attempts begin using the word 'sit' as he starts to get into position, rewarding him all the time.

Teach him to Lie Down

For some reason, this is the fastest command to teach when you do it like this and your puppy will be lying down within one training session. Simply take out his treat and hold it to his nose then move it down slowly to the floor (I usually say 'Lie Down' at this point too rather than wait until later in the training), sliding it away from him if you need to. He will start to move down. As soon as he is almost down (he won't lie down right away, and his bottom is likely to remain in mid-air) gave him the treat. Keep doing this and getting him to move further into the lie position (you can drag the treat towards you on the floor as this can often help). Reward and praise him each time. Eventually, you will only give him the treat when he is fully down. By now he will be used to your hand moving down and hearing the phrase 'Lie Down'.

Teach him to stay or wait

You can use either term with your puppy. I use both but in different circumstances. I use 'wait' when we are crossing a road and I want him to wait before I give him the command that it's ok to move. I use 'stay' if someone comes to the door and I don't want him running into the hall. You can use the same command for both of these.

To teach your dog to stay first of all ask him to sit. Then hold up your hand so that your palm is straight in front of him and directed towards his face (but not in any kind of threatening way).

Take a step backward so that you are facing him with your palm facing him and say stay. If he stays for even a few seconds, come back to him and reward him. Keep doing this while moving further away.

Leash training

At this stage of your puppy's life (up to 16-18 weeks), you won't be doing much walking outside but you can start some basic leash training if you want to. You can get him used to his leash with you holding the other end. Do this for a specific training session rather than simply putting on his leash to wander around the house. Try and do this somewhere that is not a part of the 'living' area of the home.

As soon as his leash is clipped on give him a treat. Have a treat in your hand and use this to get him to walk beside you. Hold it just in front of his nose, loosely cupped in your hand so that the palm is facing his nose with your arm hanging down beside you. He will eventually be running beside you, or more precisely, running after your hand. Build this up slowly and for no more than 5 minutes at a time at the start. Eventually, walk a few paces then turn in the opposite direction getting him to follow you. Repeat this process of walking a few steps and turning.

WHAT BREED IS RIGHT FOR YOU?

I have outlined some examples of types of dogs in the following chapter. Please remember that these are general traits of the breeds and not all dogs will behave as predicted by their breed heritage.

Some dog breeds are great with children while others prefer a quieter life. Some dogs need lots of exercise and others need hardly any at all. Do you want to hold your dog and have your dog on your lap? Do you prefer a male or female dog (I have one of both) and what are the differences, if any?

Groups of Dog types

Dogs are generally split into seven types and these are:

Sporting

Gun dogs are working dogs and were bred to accompany their owner. They are loyal and are good at retrieving. They were bred to either disturb birds or to bring them back to their owner. Examples include Spaniels. I have two spaniels and they are good at retrieving (playing fetch) but they actually never bother chasing birds or are even remotely interested in them. I know of another spaniel (the grandmother of Barney) who will jump into a lake and swim across it to follow a bird! It just means that there are no hard and fast rules.

Other examples include Retrievers - bred to retrieve the game and bring it back to the owner without damaging the game in their delicate mouth. I grew up with a retriever, fantastic with children and terrible at 'fetch' but loved to have a stick thrown. He was a beautiful gentle giant called Paddy.

Other gun dog types are Pointers and Setters and they were used to find the game and then point it out (as the name Pointer suggests).

The Sporting Group includes the American Water Spaniel, Chesapeake Bay Retriever, Cocker Spaniel, English Cocker, Curly and Flat Coat Retriever, English Setter, English, and Welsh Springer Spaniel, Pointer (German Shorthaired and German Wirehaired), Golden Retriever, Golden Setter, Irish Setter, Labrador Retriever, and the Weimaraner.

Hounds

Hound dogs fall into two types - sight hounds and scent hounds. As you would expect sighthounds hunt what they see and scent hounds hunt by using their nose. They all like to hunt as a pack.

Hound dogs, as a group, can be stubborn and very independent. They love to use their mind but don't always respond to commands. If you can keep them mentally active then this will help. They are also more likely to wander off so you need to keep an eye on them.

Scent hounds include the Basset Hound, the Beagle, and the Dachshund. They have the most sensitive noses of all dog breeds and they love the sound of their voice. They would use this to let the leader know that they are following a scent but they do tend to use their voice (bark more) even if they are not used for hunting.

Some hounds produce a unique sound known as baying. If you don't know what this sounds like then check it out before you decide to get one.

If you want a dog low on energy then the greyhound is famously lazy especially when they get a bit older. It's amazing to think that they are racing dogs yet would prefer to laze around all day.

Examples of Sighthounds include the Afghan, the Greyhound, the Irish Wolfhound, and the Whippet. Although these hounds move at speed they also love to relax. In their older years, they will happily spend the day relaxing requiring little exercise compared to other dog types.

Herding Dogs

As the name suggests, herding dogs were bred to herd and are also great at herding small children too! They are very loyal and are great family pets. These are very intelligent dogs and need lots of mental stimulation and exercise otherwise they might try to create it themselves. Examples of Herding dogs include the Border Collie and German and Australian Shepherds.

If you are also looking for a guard dog then the German Shepherd is thought to be the best. He is great for families with children but you will need to train them well. If you do, they will be incredibly obedient. They will need a lot of exercise so bear that in mind too.

Working Dogs

Working dogs have been bred for their strength and are usually larger dogs. They have worked with us for a long, long time either pulling sleds, performing rescues, or guarding our property. They are very intelligent and are great companions. However, due to their size and exercise requirements, they tend not to be ideal for families.

Examples of Working Dogs include the Akita, Bernese Mountain Dog, Boxer, Bull Mastiff, Chinook, Doberman Pinscher, Giant Schnauzer, Newfoundland, Rottweiler, Saint Bernard, and the Siberian Husky.

The Siberian Husky falls in the sub-category of pulling dogs. Pulling dogs (also the Alaskan Malamute), as the name suggests, are used to 'pulling' and they will need a great deal of exercise. They don't tend to make great pets because of this, but if you do decide on this breed, remember to get a strong harness as they are very powerful and you may find yourself getting taken for a walk rather than the other way around.

Terriers

The name terrier literally means 'dog of the earth'. They were bred as farm dogs. They chased and found foxes and other vermin. Because of this, they have a tendency to explore holes in the ground, no matter how small.

They are full of mischief, are usually excitable, and are full of energy. They make great pets but you will need to put up with their mischief and feisty personalities. They tend not to like other dogs and their wiry coats may require special grooming.

Examples of Terriers include Jack Russell, the Scottish Terrier, the Patterdale, the Cairn Terrier, the Border Terrier, and the West Highland Terrier.

Airedale, American Staffordshire Terrier, Australian Terrier, Border Terrier, Bull Terrier, Cairn Terrier, Irish Terrier, Kerry Blue Terrier, Lakeland Terrier, Miniature Schnauzer, Norfolk Terrier, Russell Terrier, Scottish Terrier, Soft Coated Wheaten Terrier, Staffordshire Bull Terrier, West Highland White Terrier, and the Wire Fox Terrier

Toy Dogs

Toy dogs, or lap dogs, were bred as companions and they adore affection and lots of petting. They have lots of energy and are very playful. They also don't tend to shed their coat so are ideal if you have an allergy or want to avoid grooming.

These dogs can become very attached to one person and are prone to separation anxiety so try to consider them and train them to cope with separation. Some of them really don't like noise and can be prone to barking (the Chihuahua).

Examples of this breed include the Bichon Frise, King Charles Spaniel, Chihuahua, the Maltese, and the Miniature Bull Terrier, the Pekingese, Pomeranian, Pug, West Highland Terrier, Shih Tzu, the Toy Poodle, and the Yorkshire Terrier.

Non-Sporting

Non-sporting dogs are dogs that do not easily fit into any other group. They are all very different in terms of size, coat, and personality.

The breeds in this group include the American Eskimo, Bichon Frise, Boston Terrier, Bulldog, Chow Chow, Dalmatian, Keeshond, Lhasa Apso, Miniature Schnauzer, Poodle, and the Tibetan Spaniel and Terrier.

Lifestyle considerations

Do you have an allergy? If you are prone to allergies then you are looking for a dog with short coats and those that tend not to shed. Toy dogs and Terriers would fit this profile. Poodles, for example, don't shed any hair. Other low-shedding breeds include the Schnauzer, Bichon Frise, Shih Tzu, and the Yorkshire Terrier.

Do you have children?

The Labrador Retrievers are well known for their loving nature and being good as part of a family. Other breeds that are great with children include the Newfoundland, Boxer, English Bulldog, and Irish Setter (as examples).

Do you have time for lots of exercise?

If you live in an apartment or you don't want to or are not able to commit to lots of exercise then you are most likely to be considering a low energy dog. Toy dogs and some types of hound e.g. a Greyhound. The Greyhound is one of the world's laziest dogs. Remember that low-energy dogs are not necessarily small dogs.

High energy dogs include the Airedale Terrier, Australian Shepherd,

Border Collie, English Springer Spaniel, Miniature Pinscher, Pointer, Siberian Husky, Staffordshire Bull Terrier, Weimaraner

How strong are you? Avoid working dogs if you can.

Do you have neighbors nearby? Avoid the dog that is prone to barking more. For example, the Scent hound group - Beagles, Bassets, and also Schnauzers.

Dog Breed Sizing, Height and Weights

As a rule of thumb here is the create sizes by dog breed size. Check with your breeder or veterinary on the likely final height and weight of your dog (some dogs can be smaller or larger than the averages noted below). This is a useful guide from Copper's Crates that is a good starting point.

Extra Small Dog Breeds 18″ – 22″ Dog Crate

Toy breeds weighing up to 10 lbs and up to 12" in height

Examples only: Boston Terrier, Chihuahua, Jack Russell, Pug, Shih Tzu

Small Dog Breeds 24″ Dog Crate

Dogs weighing between 11-25 lbs and 3"-17" in height.

Example only: King Charles Spaniel, Dachshund, French Bulldog

Medium Dog Breeds 30″ Dog Crate

Dogs weighing between 26-40 lbs and between 18"-19" in height.

Examples only: American Pit Bull Terrier, Cocker Spaniel, Dachshund, Miniature Schnauzer, Wheaten Terrier

Intermediate Dog Breeds 36″ Dog Crate

Dogs weighing between 41-70 lbs and from around 20"-22" in height.

Examples only: Alaskan Husky, Basset Hound, Beagle, Border Collie, Cocker Spaniel, English Setter, English Springer Spaniel, Siberian Husky, Standard Schnauzer, Whippet

Large Dog Breeds 42″ Dog Crate

Dogs weighing between 71-90 lbs and about 23" - 26" in height.

Examples only: Australian Shepherd, Boxer, Dalmatian, English Setter, German Shepherd, Golden Retriever, Irish Setter, Labrador Retriever, Rhodesian Ridgeback, Poodle (Standard)

Extra Large Dog Breeds 48″ Dog Crate

Dogs weighing between 91 - 110 lbs and ranging from around 26" - 28" in height

Examples only: Afghan Hound, Akita, Alaskan Malamute, Bernese Mountain Dog, Bloodhound, Doberman Pinscher, Giant Schnauzer, Greyhound

XXL Giant Dog Breeds 54″ Dog Crate

Dogs Weighing over 110 lbs and ranging from somewhere between 29" - 40" in height

Examples only: Great Dane, Irish Wolfhound, Mastiff, Newfoundland, St. Bernard

CONCLUSION

The first few weeks of having your puppy at home is both exciting and scary. Once you can get your puppy used to his crate and going outside to pee or poop then two of the most important aspects of his training and living with you will be completed. Both of these will mean that your puppy can go anywhere with you but that he will also feel safe and secure when he has to stay at home when you go out.

There are other things that you will worry about once he is home and I hope I have covered most of them in this book. Feeding and when to provide food is something I had to figure out when the puppies were little. I had never really considered what toys might be best until I had to decide which ones to get. You will forget all the annoying little aspects of this time – the mouthing and chewing is maddening at the time, but you soon forget all about it.

Of all the things I have learned over the years, the one crucial bit of advice is to remember that your puppy and your dog only want to make you and himself happy. Don't punish him when he gets things wrong, he is doing his best. Just teach him what it is that you want him to do and let him know he is on the right track by using rewards and treats. And try not to get him over-excited when you leave or return home. It really is the best way to train your puppy – and it works.

POSITIVE PUPPY OFF-LEASH RECALL TRAINING

INTRODUCTION

Recall training is the most important training that you will do with your puppy. It will reduce your stress when you take him for a walk, it will allow him to get off-leash to be able to do more exercise and have lots more freedom but, for me, the most important aspect is that good recall can also save his life.

There has been more than one occasion in the past when one of my dogs has run away from me and headed towards a road. A member of my family lost a much-loved dog like this. Another had a habit of taking off after smells and would do this in areas that were unknown to them. I know people who hate going for a walk with their dog because they feel bad about keeping her on her leash all the time because they worry about her not coming back to them.

I have a dog, Barney, and when he about 2 years old and no longer a puppy, I thought he was well enough trained. It had been hard to train a second dog outdoors and he did not get the same outdoor training as his mummy.

I didn't mind him roaming away from me, he was good at coming back, but on occasion, he would become obsessed with a smell or trying to find a ball and become completely 'deaf'. If he was a slow runner or moving slowly, I may not have worried so much about it, but he moved very fast and darted round in all directions and would never have heard me if I had called. I realized that, no matter how good he appeared to be, he had not been trained properly for recall. If I had any doubts about this, it was made very clear to me with a sharp shock when he ran in front of a car.

It was a park area with a very quiet road running through parts of it but one day a car was there. He was fine, I was not. He was very, very lucky. He has now been trained and I mention this to let you know that recall can be trained in an older dog too but I wish I had done it when he was a puppy, as I had done with Millie.

Not all dog parents want the most highly trained dog but we all need our puppies and dogs to come back when they are called and they need to do it all the time.

I can promise you that having a dog with great recall completely changes the experience of a dog walk and it becomes something to look forward to rather than fear. It is for all of these reasons that I decided to become an accredited dog trainer and I started with recall!

Recall training is one of the most difficult to get right and yet so important for all of the reasons mentioned above and it is unashamedly the main focus of this book. It takes patience and a bit of time, but in my view, it is the must-have training need for you and your puppy.

Recall training also covers the cues such as sit, stay, and of course, leash training and the recall cue itself, which in my case is 'come'. All of these fundamental cues are discussed as well as a section on leash training.

The reason recall is so difficult to train is that we are asking our dogs to stop doing something that they are enjoying and they find rewarding, and we are asking them to stop doing it and to come to us.

The only reason they will come to us instead of chasing that squirrel is if we are more interesting, rewarding, and fun.

To get to this stage, there are a few training steps that you need to do with your puppy to help with communication, reward expectation, and desired actions. You need to get him, or her, to understand what it is you want and need them to do.

Some of the training methods are simple and some will require a bit of training on your part. You will also need to know what equipment you are going to need and this is detailed in the first chapter.

The training is split into 3 main areas - the first stage is indoor training, then outside the house in enclosed areas and finally, in the park.

To understand why the following training is effective, it is useful to understand a little bit about dogs and to dispel a common myth.

Dogs don't adhere to the dominance or alpha models we were told about in the past. For example, walking in front of us, or trying to get into the house or car first, is not a sign that they are showing their dominance over us or trying to dominate us - it's just a sign that they want to get somewhere quickly and we are too slow. If we don't want them to do these things then we need to let them know what behavior we want and then reward them for doing it so that it becomes what they want to do too.

It is now well evidenced that reward, or positive reinforcement is an effective training method and is more likely to succeed than punishment. A relaxed puppy learns faster. Using punishment as a training technique increases stress, can make training harder and longer, and can lead to other types of behavior problems.

I use positive reinforcement training, we want our puppy to want to do something, not only is it effective but the smile and joy you will receive from your puppy is often the best moment of every day.

This all means that it is important to reward the desired action of your puppy all the time and as soon as it occurs, to clearly show the relationship between a behavior and a reward. If you leave it too late, he simply won't understand why he is getting a reward. Try to bear this in mind as you read this book.

You are going to learn about cues, markers, and rewards and all of these will be used for every training setup that you do with your puppy.

Finally, your puppy will get bored. This means try to keep your training session to between 10 and 20 minutes for best effect - you can always return to it again later but remember to end each session with success. If he just isn't understanding what you want him to do, end the session with something you know he can do so that he feels great and manages to achieve his reward.

PREPARATION

What's in a name?

Your puppy will already have a name, but if you are reading this before you have your puppy, then it's good to know that the name of your puppy can actually make training easier.

The best names end with a vowel sound (dogs 'hear' at a higher frequency range than we do and so this grabs the attention better) and start with a hard letter sound like B or D rather than perhaps Happy (we had a dog called Happy).

Ideally, their name should contain two syllables and you want to avoid any names that they might confuse with a cue.

I named Millie before I knew about dog names and it probably isn't the perfect training name but she is Millie and she trained really well so name tips are just something to bear in mind.

Try and say the name a few times too, you need to make sure all members of the family are happy to use it in the park. My sister has a dog called Tootsie and our brother wasn't too comfortable calling for her. But the name suited her so her name is still Tootsie - 14 years later.

Don't worry if you take a day or two to find just the right name that seems to fit who your puppy is. I had named Barney, Ben for around 5 days before I decided it just didn't suit him. If you have a dog from a shelter and you really want to change his name or don't know what his name used to be, then give him a few days to get used to it (but it might take him a bit longer).

To get him used to his name say it and reward him when you say it even when there is no response. Then, as soon as there is a response, immediately reward with a tastier treat. Just walk around the house and say his name and reward his response. Getting your puppy used to their name can be fun for us all.

Focus and attention: 'Look at me'

Before you start taking your puppy outside for walks you will want to teach him to look at you. To do this he needs to want to pay attention to you. As an aside, this is great during training. If your puppy starts to get engrossed or fixated on something then get him to look at you - it changes his focus back to you. I find this particularly useful for leash training.

Simply reward him every time he looks at you and repeat the process in many different locations and environments. You can reward him with click-treat, with praise and reward and the reward might be some play or a toy (spaniels love a ball throw).

Training your puppy to look at you can be done with an easy game and it will teach your puppy to look and also get him used to his name.

To play the game, sit down with your puppy with a handful of treats in your pocket. Make sure that you are sitting so that you are close to him but that he needs to look up to see your eyes.

Take out a treat and get his attention. You can get his attention by making a sound or squeaking a toy. Place the treat between your eyes. Your puppy will follow the treat all the way to your eyes. You will probably burst out laughing but don't worry about that, he will wiggle into you for a cuddle. You might need to start again though. But don't forget to give him his treat!

Once you start again, place the treat between your eyes and as soon as he has eye contact with you, even briefly give him his treat. In the beginning, the eye contact might be an accident on his part but that's okay. If he gets rewarded for it, he will soon learn. Keep repeating until he always has eye contact with you.

Keep doing this and then start putting the treat behind your head or neck but try and get eye contact before you give him his treat. If he doesn't look at you at first, then help him find your eyes so that he knows what he is supposed to do.

The next part of this game is to start using his name. Do exactly the same process but as you place the treat between your eyes, say his name. You will need to do all this quite quickly to link the eye contact and name call with his reward but he will get there.

He now knows that when you say his name you want him to look at you and to pay attention to you because there will be a reward coming!

Equipment

You are now going to need a few tools and some quipment to progress with all the training. Here are the main items you will be using in this training:

Treats

Treats are the mainstay of dog training. When you first start out you will be horrified at how fast they disappear.

Some people cut up hot dogs, I made something called liver cake (it worked really well), and one of the simplest things to do is to grab a handful of his kibble to use as a dog training treat.

Kibble isn't always seen by your dog as being of high value so work out what his preferred treats are and which ones he loves most. Just remember that it is important to use more than one treat, try and have a selection of at least 3 or 4 if you can.

Then, depending on what you want him to do and how much he might not immediately understand or want to do it, use the treat that matches his effort. For example, if he absolutely loves cheese then save this as a special treat, if he has learned to sit then offer him kibble when he sits. If he is doing recall and takes ages to return then he gets kibble, if he returns quickly, he gets the cheese. This process can increase the connection between you and your puppy as you start to understand each other.

There are a few reasons that treats might not work. They might not be tasty enough, your puppy might not be hungry (try and train him on an empty stomach), he might be too stressed or he might get a treat all the time so he doesn't realize what the reward means.

Over reinforcement, which simply means using treats too often, is common.

This is why, over time, you will reduce the value of the treat for the same learned behavior and reward based on the quality of the response. You are eventually aiming to have the desired behavior with no treats at all (you won't always be able to have a treat in your hand) but you will always praise your dog for returning to you and you may also have a reward game for him to play (a tug or a ball to throw). The reward might not always be a treat and it doesn't need to be. A dog can never have too much love or too much play.

Some dogs are not food-orientated, and in this case, find toys that he likes. Just like the treats, try and establish which ones have the most value and which have the least value. For Barney, the highest value toy is a ball, and I know that on many occasions, he would prefer a ball to a treat. A ball is often used for training sniffer dogs or rescue dogs.

Dogs train better when they are making their own choices and you want him to want to make the choice to come to you when you ask him. This equally means that you must never be angry when he comes back to you, no matter how long it has taken. Coming back to someone who might be angry is not enticing and is worth avoiding.

Harness

Collars and choke collars are no longer thought to be good for dogs. They can be worn in the house but harnesses should be used for training - especially leash and recall. Training is all about trust and restrictive items just won't build the trust you are looking for.

If your puppy jumps around when you try to get the harness on him, a trick is to begin by holding a treat through the opening of his harness where you need his head to go through and encouraging him to put his head through to get the treat. You need to deal with his legs so ask him to sit as you do this. I use 'sit' and 'wait' as I pull the straps around his chest and under his legs. He usually stands (I just use the 'wait' cue for this part) for the lower strap. He just seems to find this more comfortable.

Reward each step and success and take it slowly.

Leash

Avoid flexible leashes. They won't give you the control that you need and they get tangled up in legs - all sorts of legs. You will ideally want to use a long-leash (around 25ft-30ft in length). This is known as a long-line. You will also want a shorter training leash. His day-leash or 'normal' leash will be shorter than the training leash. A 4ft leash can work well as both a training and a day leash.

Try and get one with a circular ring on the handle so that you can use this to clip the leash and collar together to create a holding cord if you need it. I found this extremely useful as I could clip Millie to a table leg if we were out without removing her leash completely.

Whistles and Clickers

Almost all leash training will involve using a clicker or a marker of some form. I train with and without a clicker. Whistles are great for recall especially for dog breeds that like to explore. With clicker training, this must always be followed with a reward, for example, click-treat. This is known as the primary and secondary enforcer. Eventually, you will click less and less as the behavior is established but you must always follow a click with a treat.

Toys

You are going to use your puppy's toys during the recall training. You are going to try to get him to leave a toy and come to you when he is called. You will have a treat so that he sees the value of leaving his toy and coming to get something else he loves.

If you are training a gun dog for retrieval then you can get lots of scent items such as rabbit scent balls and puppy dummies. We once trained a spaniel by scenting a sock with a pheasant and hiding it for them to find when asked to fetch.

THE FOUNDATIONAL CUES

Essentially you are aiming to have your dog return to you on cue no matter how many other exciting things are going on around him. This means that you want your puppy to want to return to you on cue not only when there are no other dogs around, but also when there are other dogs to play with. You can only achieve this if you are more interesting than whatever else he is doing and if he is listening and paying attention to you.

In summary, you want him to stop what he is doing; you want him to look at you, and you want him to come to you on cue.

Like many things with training, it takes a little bit of time. Ideally, you want your dog to automatically return to you whenever he feels threatened. This means any bad situation can be avoided before it even begins.

Sit-stay is an important part of recall training and it's important as a part of overall behavior. Ideally, every time he sees another dog you will want to get him to come to you and sit and stay. Barney was great at the first part, but the sit-stay began with an attempt to jump into my arms.

You will start the recall and sit-stay training at home and won't let him off leash outside in an unenclosed area until you are happy that he will return to you, and you are confident that he is doing what you want him to do in the home or the garden.

To do this, you will need to introduce different locations and then introduce lots of distractions as the training develops because there will be lots of exciting activity and scents in the park but wait until his recall is up to about 70%-80% before you start adding the distraction element of his recall training.

Decide on your cue

Most people use the word 'come' or 'here' as their vocal cue for their dog. Once you have decided on the word you want to use then you must keep it. Consistency is vital for your dog to understand what you mean.

You will start using this early. When you want him to come for his dinner you will use it, when you are going to give him a big cuddle or play with him, you will use it. The word itself doesn't mean anything to your dog but the outcome of his action means he feels great and gets something he loves. In training language, he is building a positive association with the word.

Keep the training around 10 minutes and watch out for any signs that he is getting stressed (quick head movements, grabbing the treat/food, ears flat), and try not to get him over-excited. If your puppy is a part of a household then get all members involved in the training too. At the end of his training get him to do something you know he can do so that it ends in success. You want him to enjoy his training.

Sit-Stay and Release

Sit-stay is one of the most important cues your dog will learn. Dogs naturally want to follow you, especially as you move away from them.

You will want to use both noise (vocal, whistle, or squeaky toy) and visual cues. Be slightly careful of the squeaky toy. Millie, after her pups were born, heard a squeak and ran to protect the toy. Depending on your dog, it might be more of a distraction, rather than helping to focus attention.

Your visual cue will be holding up your hand as if you are directing traffic to stop but without raising your arm - just hold it in from of you and directing your palm to your puppy's face. This is the stay visual cue. The verbal cue would be 'Stay'. Visual cues are also a good way of helping your dog focus on you.

Normally the first part is to ask your puppy to 'sit' then this is followed by 'stay' (or 'wait').

By the stage that you are going for outside walks, you will have already trained your puppy to 'sit' and will have practiced 'stay' in the home and garden over his first few weeks at home.

To recap on the 'sit' training you will have already done - never force your puppy to sit by putting your hand on his lower back and pushing it down.

Decide on your visual signal for sit. An example would be to hold out your hand palm facing-up, then gently move your fingers upwards as if you are 'lifting' his head with your four fingers.

Take out a treat and bring it towards your puppy's nose slowly moving it up over his head so that he naturally goes into a sit position. I tend to hold the treat in a similar way to the hand movement that I am going to use as the visual signal. As soon as his bottom touches the ground praise him and give him the treat. If you are clicker training then use the clicker as his bottom touches the ground and provide the treat.

Try to make sure that you provide the praise/treat when he is sitting and not when he has moved to a standing position.

Whenever you see your puppy sit praise and reward him (with voice or clicker - click-treat) and then start introducing the verbal cue. You can start the verbal cue earlier, for example, say the cue 'sit' right before his bottom touches the ground and he is due to receive his praise/reward.

Every time after that, when your puppy sits try and remember to praise/reward them as this will build this into a behavior default. One that they enjoy and know brings praise/reward and they are comfortable and safe with.

You will want your puppy to sit for lots of reasons. In the car, when you go to the door, at a crosswalk, and so on. This means you need to train him to sit but you also need to let him know when it's okay to move forward.

To do this, start with him on his leash. Get him to sit (and reward) then decide on your cue for 'let's go' this can be 'let's go' or 'ok go' or whatever you choose. Say your cue and move a few steps and praise him, ask him to sit and reward. Begin with short distances (a few steps) to get him used to the 'ok go' cue. Repeat the process of 'sit', reward, 'ok go', reward, walk a few steps then repeat. This is known as the release command or release cue. This can mean that the release cue is seen as a reward too. Your puppy comes back and then gets to go and have fun again. It also means that he will learn that coming back doesn't mean there will be no more play.

Finally, some trainers consider recall to include holding your puppy's collar when he returns as a full recall and used before the release cue. The puppy comes back, he sits and the collar is taken then the reward is given. This is followed by the release cue.

Some are happy with only the sit. This really is up to you but I prefer the collar hold as it gives you more control should you ever need it.

RECALL TRAINING STEPS

You will begin teaching your puppy what you mean by the recall cue. I will use the example of 'come'. The important part is to always use this word and use it only when you want him to come to you. This means that you don't want to mix it into other cues. This one word means one thing and one thing only - to come to you. You will adopt this rule for all his cues. Make sure each one is unique to the action expected and not mixed into other meanings or cues. For example, don't use 'come here' if 'here' is used as another cue.

Start your recall training in the house then move to enclosed areas with few distractions. I know of someone who trained for recall in their hallway which was ideal for ensuring their puppy was set up for success during the early training - there were limited direction options and little distraction. This is important. You want to ensure that your puppy always succeeds and this might mean you need to adapt things to make sure that he can succeed through each step of his training.

Get him used to coming to you

Once you have decided on your location, show your puppy his

favorite treat or toy, and as he comes towards you to get his toy or treat (don't ask him to just let him do it by himself), praise him and reward him as he reaches you. Do this a few times.

After a few times start to add in his cue so that he gets used to it. As he starts coming towards you to get his toy (and ideally looks at you), add in the cue you have chosen. In my example, 'Come'.

Once he is doing this you can add in a sit.

As soon as he comes to you give him his treat and ask him to sit. When he sits give him another reward.

You then want to keep repeating this game in other rooms of the house and with more distractions.

One way to do this is to have other family members or friends in the room. As you walk towards them and he starts to get interested in this interesting and fun distraction, quickly run away and call him so that he chases you. Encourage him to catch up and when he does, he will receive his treat and probably a big cuddle as an extra reward.

Like many of the games, you can play with him, mix them up so that he doesn't always know what to expect. It will keep him even more interested in what you are about to get up to next.

10 steps for basic recall

1. Decide on your location (hallway, kitchen, etc)
2. Show your puppy his favorite toy or a treat but don't call him, let him come to you
3. When he gets to you give him his reward.
4. Repeat
5. Start adding your recall cue as he starts coming towards you so that he gets to know it
6. Reward him when he gets to you
7. Repeat steps 5 and 6
8. When he comes to you give him his treat then ask him to sit

and give him another treat (so that he knows that when he comes to you, you want him to sit)

9. Repeat this until he knows what to do
10. Repeat the recall and sit training in other locations and start to add in distractions

Training sit-stay

Ask your puppy to sit, then 'stay' and still facing him, take a few steps backward holding up your hand in the 'stay' position. Walk back to your puppy and reward him. Do this a few times and then take a few more steps backward increasing the distance then walk back to him and reward him. Keep repeating moving further away. Your puppy is learning that not only is he getting rewarded but that you come back to him. Start to move to different positions so that you are to each side and eventually behind him. If he gets up, just move back to him and give him praise then try again.

You will need to repeat this in several different locations, and in all the different positions, to the front of him, behind him, etc., and not only in one room but in a lot of rooms, as well as in your garden or enclosed area and all the different parts of them. As he starts to get better at this, introduce more distractions and start moving behind objects so that he can't see you. Try and do this everywhere you go.

Sit-stay come

This was the main recall training I started with Millie indoors when she was around 14 weeks old and it was very effective.

Ask your puppy to sit and then asked her to stay as above (I used the word 'wait' and held my hand up).

Walk backward a few steps facing your puppy - I kept holding my hand up as I was walking away.

The difference now is that you want him to come to you following the sit-stay. If he stays for just a few seconds, ask him to come and give him a treat and be delighted with him.

Keep repeating this and do it at the start of every training session. As he starts to get good at this, start to move further and further away and eventually try walking away with your back to him.

Build up distance and distractions to this game - but if you go too far and he starts to come towards you too soon, just go back a few steps to the point at which it was working and then keep trying to build the distance.

The next stage is to go outside for a walk. You can go for a walk on-leash, but not off-leash until you have proofed his recall training.

Going Outside - enclosed area

Training for recall outside of the house is vital. It is here where he is going to find the most distractions. You must make sure the area you choose in enclosed. Just like the early days of house training, you will start with very few distractions. This is when you are going to work with the clicker and training leads and when you will start working out the value in which he holds each of his treats.

A great tip is to train your puppy before he has eaten - this means the treat you are offering will be of higher value to him and he will be more interested in them! And don't train him for too long. Pay attention if he looks like he is getting bored and stop the training and start again the next day.

You also want him to know that coming to you is more rewarding than doing something else - it is exciting and fun and may involve a tasty treat. I also used to crouch down and hold my arms wide as Barney ran to me when he was a puppy. It wasn't meant as a signal but even today if I hold my arms wide, he will come to me.

To get started, put your puppy in his harness and on his training leash. Just like the early indoor training you can start with rewarding an action with no other cues to get him used to the long-line and outdoor training. He will know what to do quickly because he has already been trained indoors.

The difference is now you are going to place something he might want to eat, or play with, a short distance away from him and within the length of the leash (or just a bit further away). You are now introducing something he wants to get to that is away from you.

As he goes towards the object or his treat (but not too tasty), tighten his leash and say his name then the cue e.g., Barney 'come'. As soon as he turns and comes (only a step or two) reward and praise him. If you are using a clicker, you will click as soon as he turns (there is more on clicker training later). Aim to have an even tastier treat for him than the one he was going towards. You want to increase the value of the treats the more you want him to do something so that he prefers to choose that treat.

By having the leash on him you can also gently encourage him to come towards you to get his reward if you need to. The leash helps you have a bit of control over this recall in the early stages as he learns the cue 'come' before he starts to outside where he will want to explore.

Another game to play on the leash that helps him learn is quite simple. Give him a few treats, then run forward or backward for a few steps, and say 'Barney, Come!' in a playful voice. Hold the treat out as the height of his nose (so all his feet are on the ground) and as he reaches you give him his treat. You are using his name to get his attention, not as a cue.

You can extend this game to add the sit. As he reaches you for his treat move the treat up in front of his nose so that he is forced back into a sit position to get his treat. In this way the come and sit are the same cue which means when you ask him to come, he will come to you and sit without being asked to sit. He will start to become familiar with this because you always ask him to do this when he comes to you.

You can, and should start practicing this as soon as you can. Puppies learn most up to the age of 16 weeks.

The next step for recall training is to have him move further away from you and for him to return when he hears his cue. Good recall means he does this all the time. If he is not, then he is not ready and you won't want to risk letting him off-leash. This is best done outdoors on a long line.

To understand what you are asking your puppy to do, think about it like this. He is exploring and having fun, he is finding interesting and exciting things to sniff and play with. When you call him, you want him to prefer to come to you rather than to do whatever he is doing. If you can achieve this then there is no reason for him not to return to you when called.

To do this you will want to start with training games, and you will want to have worked out what his favorite treats or toys are and which ones top the list. Cheese, hotdog, carrot, kibble - my two dogs love cheese and I used the make liver cake which they absolutely loved. It was probably the single reason Millie's recall and leash training went so well.

Using the long-line

You don't need to use the long-line but it can be really helpful and, if you can, I would recommend it. To describe how this is done I picked a hand but you will end up doing something that works for you.

Practice this in a garden if you can and one without distractions at the start. You want to get used to working with the long line and you also want to test that your training is working.

Hold the end of the line on your right hand so that you have it tightly held. Wrap the length of the line into loops so that you can slowly release the line over the front of your body and through your left hand to let your puppy move further away when you want him to and hold this in the same hand making sure it can be easily released.

This means that in your left hand you are holding the part of the line that is acting as your dog leash and is attached to his harness - but your hand is operating as a feeder, controlling the delivery of the line.

You will have your right hand holding the end of the long line as well as the loops of the spare line and in the other - your left hand - you will be feeding the line gently through it. This means you can slowly release the line through your left hand or clamp it closed (gently) to stop further release of the line.

Once you are comfortable you can start the training.

Slowly move in a circle on the same spot so that he is running around you, loosening the line so that he can move away from you and then call him back to you. Just get him used to the leash and watching you and so that he knows he gets a reward when he comes to you.

You can then add another game (and later you can play this off-leash too) by throwing a treat away from you and letting your puppy run towards the treat. Once he has eaten the treat, call his name to get his attention. Wait until he looks at you, then as soon as he does use the clicker (click) and say the cue, 'come', and when he comes to you give him praise and his reward. You will then throw another treat in a different direction and repeat this quite a few times so that he is running away and towards you and always with the click marker (if you are using a clicker), and come cue, in a fun game.

When you want to 'pull', or need to do so, to encourage him to come back on his cue then move or lean forward rather than move against him and gently make the line shorter. This means that you are in control of your puppy whilst also allowing him to return and move away easily so that he can move around without feeling 'pulled'.

The final part is to wait until he is preoccupied with something and is not looking at you. Get his attention and ask him to come. If he comes then praise and reward. If he doesn't come, just walk to him and show him all the treats you have, and walk away from him. He is likely to follow you to try and get a treat. Just ignore him. As soon as he is not right beside you, ask him to come. When he does, give him lots of praise and a favorite treat. It won't take long for him to realize that coming is much better than not coming.

You will now repeat the indoor sit-stay come training in the outdoor environment. Just as you did indoors, get your puppy to sit-stay and then move away from him while still facing him and then ask him to 'come'. Slowly build the distance but keep using the longline.

The next two steps are new and before you can try off-leash outdoor you want to introduce the 'go play' cue which combines the sit-stay.

Ask him to sit-stay beside you, then use your release cue, 'go play', and start walking. As he moves away and then moves ahead of you, call him back to you (click on a turn of the head towards you if he pays attention to his name), as he starts coming towards you might want to encourage him (I held my arms open but you can also click), reward when he gets to you, then ask him to sit and give him another reward.

The last step is to practice off-leash - again, you will do this in a space that is enclosed and where he will be safe. Simply let him wander away from you and then call him to you using your cue. Be exciting and have a treat ready for him. Try and keep his attention on you as he comes to you - make a noise or hold your arms open - you want him to be focused on you.

Don't keep repeating the cue if he doesn't come or start raising your voice. This will confuse him and he won't be able to understand what his cue word is, eventually tuning it out which means he just won't hear it. If you raise your voice, he won't think that coming to you is going to be lots of fun. Eventually, it could have the opposite effect, and he won't want to come at all.

The best way to train your puppy is using random and variable reinforcement. All this means is that over time change how often he gets a treat for the same behavior so that he is hoping for it each time (don't wait too long to reward as you start to reduce the level of treats) and change the value of the treat (for a really good response).

If you want to, you can measure the average response time for recall (either daily or per 12 returns, etc.) so that when he comes back faster, he gets a super tasty treat. This is the most effective way to train your puppy to become addicted to coming back to you.

One last trick - if your puppy has taken a while to return on cue then as he arrives show him the treat and put it back in your pocket. As he moves away, ask him to 'come' and when he gets to you give him his treat. This will help him learn that acting right away gets the reward.

Using a Clicker

Clicker training is useful when you want to mark the correct behavior of your puppy at the exact moment he starts to respond. As I have already mentioned, if you are doing click-reward then it must always be followed by a reward but the reward and the timing of the reward varies.

In the beginning, all you need to do is get your puppy used to the click-reward (at the start you will use a treat). Keep repeating click-treat. He doesn't have to do anything at this stage as you are just getting him used to the clicker marker which means a reward is coming.

Slowly reduce the time between the click and the treat and vary the gaps - he will still expect the treat and he will know that it is coming but it might not happen right away.

Once he gets good at this you will be able to click without the treat and vary the reinforcement by using his favorite toy or a quick game that he likes.

For example, when you call his name and he begins to start coming towards you, you can click so that he knows a reward is coming. It helps to keep him motivated to come all the way back to you in the expectation of a good time when he gets there.

Recall Summary and where the Clicker fits in

If you are using a clicker as a marker then the full process would look like this:

1. Get your puppy to come to you

Start by throwing a treat away from you then throw a treat at your feet. Reward every time your puppy comes back to you for any reason. You can add the click with your clicker to mark as soon as he turns towards you.

2. Add a cue

As your puppy turns towards, again this is for any reason, add your recall cue (and your click if you are using a clicker to mark or capture the behavior). The recall cue can be 'come', 'here' or a whistle - either your own whistle or use a plastic one.

Practice at different locations and over different distances before you move to the next step.

3. As soon as your puppy looks towards you click and add the recall cue. As you are walking on the leash vary the length. Every time he looks towards your click and add the recall cue (and don't forget the reward).

4. You will now cue him to look and come to you. With your puppy walking in front of you say (or whistle) your cue, as he turns towards you add the click marker. Practice by varying the distance and the speed the dog is moving away.

5. If you want to add a sit then this is when you will add it to your training.

When he arrives back to you use your sit cue to get him to sit. As soon as he sits add a click and then the reward.

6. Add a collar hold. You can train this as a separate item or you can add it into the recall process here.

When he has arrived back and sits, lean in and take hold of his collar - as you do this use your clicker to mark then reward.

Once he is good and is succeeding with steps 1 to 6 you can start adding in distractions.

You will start with low-level distractions and build them up to higher-value distractions.

Distractions might be kibble, bread, eggs, cheese, meat, and toys (again in order of least to most favorite).

As he moves towards the distraction e.g., the bread, start your recall with your recall cue and the click-reward process above. If he fails then reduce the value of the distraction until he is succeeding.

In terms of what distractions might be, then this can be a dog he knows, a dog he doesn't know (high-value distraction), someone he knows, a group of people, a jogger, a bicycle an old scent, and the high-value new scent (a squirrel that you have noticed running up a tree).

Try and remember to complete a sequence. Try to always have your dog notice you (click), come to you (encouragement) arrive (treat), sit (treat), collar hold (treat), 'go play' (reward). This is much more rewarding than 'come', treat, end of the game.

By continuing to award after he comes back to you, by rewarding the sit, collar hold and then releasing with a 'go play', he will have the expectation of more exciting things to come than if the rewards ended with the return cue only and he also knows he can return to playing after if he comes back to you and receives all his rewards and treats. Don't forget that the 'go play' is a reward in itself.

This will become even more useful once you start going outdoors to parks and other walks where there are even more exciting distractions.

There is one last piece of training that you want to do before you go off-leash to the park and this is often missed out but is the training that can make all the difference.

Emergency stop

Training for an emergency stop can be one aspect of recall that saves your dog's life. It is also quite easy to train especially once you have been working on recall training.

First of all, you will want to use a specific cue. This can be any word but, again, it can only have one meaning. The most common word that is used is 'Stop'. Just make sure this is not used as a part of any other cue.

To begin with, have your puppy or dog sitting in front of you and have a treat in your hand. If your dog is not food orientated try using one of his toys.

Take a step back put your arm in the air as if you are trying to stop the traffic or saying hello to someone who is a distance away. This is important as it is more likely that your emergency stop signal will be visual as well as sound-based (call or whistle to get attention) when your dog is a distance away from you.

Raise your arm with the treat in the hand of this arm, say the word 'Stop', and then throw the treat over your dog's head towards his rear from your raised hand so that the treat falls behind him or just beside him. You want to make sure that your dog needs to turn around to get the treat.

As he starts to return to you, repeat by putting your arm in the air, saying Stop and throwing another treat over his head. You will notice that he starts to pay attention to you and your hands which is what you want him to do. Once he is paying attention, turning to get the treat and stopping to turn again as you say raise your arm, say stop and throw the next treat you can think about increasing the distance but if there are any problems with the next step return to this first stage.

You will now start throwing the treat a bit further away so that there is a bigger distance between you so that when you say Stop, put your arm in the air and throw the treat over his head he is not close to you. This is how you can build up the long-distance emergency stop.

Try to make sure the treat doesn't land in front of him because you want him to turn around to get the treat. You want him to do this because it stops his forward movement. Keep building up the distance and repeating the exercise.

You want to reach the point where, with your arm in the air, you say Stop and he looks towards you and stops. If he starts to come towards you, go back to the first step and reinforce the stop when he is right in front of you.

If your dog is a fast learner, it may take a few days but can take a few weeks so just be patient.

The very last step, before final proofing, is when you don't throw the treat at the end but instead, walk towards him to give him his reward. This is because, if you are in a park and he is far away you won't be able to throw a treat behind him and so he needs to know that a reward is coming once you reach him.

Proofing

As you go through your training you will want to prove at each stage. At the very end, you will want to prove everything together.

Proofing is when you want to prove to yourself that the training has worked. You will proof before you let your puppy off-leash.

To do this, you will create distractions and then aim to get him to come to you on cue.

You should also proof around other dogs. Try and arrange a play-date with at least one other dog and then while he is playing with them (and still on the long-line) call him to you. Make sure you have a very tasty treat and be full of praise when he comes to you.

This particular activity is also useful to teach him that coming to you doesn't mean the end of the play. Once he comes to you and receives his reward he is released to his cue, such as 'let's go', to play again.

The last step is to practice off-leash - again, you will do this in a space that is enclosed and where he will be safe. Simply let him wander away from you and then call him to you using your cue. Be exciting and have a treat ready for him.

Don't keep repeating the cue if he doesn't come or start raising your voice. This will confuse him and he won't be able to understand what his cue word is. If you raise your voice, he won't think that coming to you is going to be lots of fun. Eventually, it could have the opposite effect and he won't want to come at all.

Now that he is proofed, you are ready to take him to the park off-leash to meet new sounds, smells, people, and other dogs.

GOING TO THE PARK

You can take your puppy to the park on a long line but never let him off-leash until you are confident of his recall. You can let go of the long leash and if he runs too far ahead of you, you can stand on the end of it. It is much easier to do this than try and grab a shorter lead.

As you start to venture out on walks, your puppy won't be the only one meeting other similar animals to talk and play with. It's important to pay attention to your puppy and to keep playing with him, and being fun, during a walk too.

Standing around and talking to other dog walkers and ignoring him will mean, although he might be well exercised by all his running around, he is learning that you are not the most exciting thing in the park and his attention to you (and your recall cue) may not be heard. He will simply tune it out because his attention is elsewhere.

Once you are ready to move to the park and encounter even more distractions you will want to begin with using high value (or higher value) treats than you have been using indoors and in the enclosed area. It is going to be harder for him to return and therefore you want his reward to be extra special. You will also vary these treats so he doesn't know what to expect but he knows a really tasty treat is coming.

You might also want to vary the timing of the treat so he knows it's coming and it will be tasty but it might be a 1, 2, or 5 seconds (you will want to start varying immediacy of the reward when you are doing the outdoor enclosed training).

Try not to only call your dog to you at the end of his walk. If you do it throughout the walk and reward him each time he comes back he won't associate recall with the end of playtime. At the end of the walk make coming back fun and rewarding rather than something he doesn't like. I tend to play more at the end of the walk as I return to the entry gate of the park.

During the walk you can vary his treat reward depending on how well he comes back to you when you give him his recall cue. If you call and he continues to do what he is doing for a minute or two and then comes back, don't reward him right away.

Let him smell his treat and then let him start to move away from you. Call him again quickly (you want him to be set up to succeed, he needs to know what you want him to), and if he immediately turns around and comes back then reward and praise him. He will then be able to learn exactly what you mean and want from him when you give him his recall cue.

In the early stages try rewarding him with one of his least favorite treats if he takes his time to come back and a nicer one if he comes back quickly. This ensures that he doesn't think he is being punished (by not getting his treat) for coming back even if he took his time about it.

But remember, if you are already interesting, and you have established your connection with your puppy this will be much easier.

Reinforcing the recall training

It doesn't matter where you are with your puppy or dog you always want to try and keep reinforcing and rewarding his behavior especially his recall.

As he gets used to recall you can start varying the reward and the time of the reward.

Let him run ahead and then recall and do this at different distances. Test him with scents outdoors too. Find an old scent and let him sniff at it and then call him. Don't forget to get his attention then add the cue. As soon as he starts to come to you and away from the scent encourage him to return to you and give him his reward and then his sit-stay and release. You then want to find a more recent scent and you will want to watch out for a squirrel or a rabbit disappearing into the undergrowth so that you know it's a new scent. This is much harder for a dog to leave. Repeat the recall but this time make the reward of more value.

Keep playing games outdoors that continue to reinforce recall too. I have given some ideas for games at the end of this chapter.

Other dogs and their communication signals

The first thing that is going to happen when you are able to take your puppy out for real walks after his vaccinations is that he is going to meet other dogs.

Your puppy is going to be playful and excited to meet other dogs but these dogs may not be so eager to have an excited puppy trying to play with them. Older dogs (those over 2 years old) are not likely to want to play. Dogs over 2 years old will tend to only play with dogs they know after this age and many will stop playing with other dogs altogether. Both Millie and Barney don't play with other dogs anymore, they run along together or play with their balls or sticks.

You will also need to pay attention to how the dogs you meet are reacting. Dogs will tell you far in advance if they are getting annoyed or are uncomfortable or feel threatened. I don't know how many times I have seen the owner of a dog watch as his dog tries to get another dog to play and that dog tries, again and again, to say 'no' until eventually, it runs out of options and snaps at the dog who is pestering it.

These are the general stages to watch out for, and this will be the case both for your dog and for dogs you meet. Try to pay attention to what dogs are telling each other and telling us.

If a dog is displaying this behavior, then these are signs that he is feeling threatened and is not happy with the attention of another dog when it is close to him: -

Stage 1: Yawning, looking away, licking lips, moving away

Stage 2: Panting, hackles up, and whale eyes (when a dog shows the whites of his eyes). This is a clear warning signal. If this still doesn't work then the next part will be a lip curl or snarl

Stage 3: Lip curl or snarl or growl and possibly a snap. Then finally we will reach the stage we don't want to be

Stage 4: A lunge towards the other dog (or the source of the 'threat') with barking as your dog tries to make the threat go away and then this may be followed by a bite.

How dogs greet each other

In terms of what you need to be aware of when you meet other dogs is to watch them and understand what they are saying.

A dog running at another dog is not going to go down well. I am still surprised how often I see dog owners letting their dogs do this. Both Millie and Barney are friendly dogs but they hate it. If you see a dog running towards your puppy or dog then there are a few things you can do.

As soon as I see this happening, and depending on how far away the other dog is and how fast they are running, I will throw a ball or a stick to distract Millie and Barney. This can sometimes encourage the other dog as well and if I notice this, I just ignore the other dog and turn away with Millie and Barney and walk in the opposite direction. If Barney is playing further away from me and he feels threatened by another dog he comes back to me to be safe and if a dog runs towards him, he comes as close as he can - he sometimes still tries to jump up into my arms.

Millie tends to feel less threatened and seems to find it easier to deal with other dogs without resorting to aggression or fear. She must communicate well! And she does this by a lip curl, then a growl, sometimes she adds in a whale eye, then an air snap but all of this is extremely unusual and she needs a lot of provocation. She always, like most dogs, starts with avoidance of the other dog if she can.

Others signs to watch out for include tails, are the tails up, and are the hackles up? Neither necessarily mean that the dog is aggressive but it indicates high adrenaline. If you notice this distract your puppy or dog away from the other dog.

Two dogs that meet each other head-on and stare into each other's faces are not being friendly but a dog that approaches from the side is being polite and asking for the intrusion into your dog's space. A face greeting followed by a bottom sniff tends to be friendly. Bottom sniffing, generally, is fine and nothing to worry about. If another dog puts his head across another dogs' shoulders this can be a sign of aggression and it can often be followed by mounting. This is not a good sign.

Just remember to always ask another dog owner if it is ok for your puppy or dog to play with their dog. Do this especially if their dog is on a leash. Don't forget a dog that is on a leash might feel threatened by another dog, who is not on a leash, and who then tries to play with him. The dog on the leash will feel constrained and this can lead to anxiety and a reaction to defend himself.

All of this is very important as your puppy begins his first walks. The experiences he has with other dogs at this stage are vital to how he views other dogs in the future, and if his experience is negative, then he can easily build a negative association with other dogs - and be aggressive himself because he would see them as a threat.

One of the ways that you can help keep your puppy from getting over-excited around other dogs is to be more exciting yourself! Of course, you can also teach him sit-stay. Every time he sees another dog you will want to get him to come to you and sit and stay. You will already have been training this, so keep doing it in the park and off-leash, and reward and praise him at each stage as he responds to his cues. Every time he learns a little bit more, click and reward.

Of course, as you first start to take your puppy out, he is likely to want to run up to other dogs himself. This is very different as it will be clear to most dogs that he is not being aggressive but curious and playful. He is a puppy after all. However, as noted earlier, dogs older than 2 years old don't tend to like being harassed by a puppy so just make sure you don't create a situation that then leads your puppy to start fearing other dogs. Millie, who is now 11 years old and has been a mum herself, will persevere with a puppy for a few minutes but she will then let it know to leave her alone. Barney (now 5 years old) will try to completely ignore a puppy for as long as he can.

However, puppies learn by meeting other dogs, and by learning how far they can go without a warning, so the socialization you will have done will have helped them but make sure you keep introducing them to other dogs, starting with ones you know.

How to interact with humans

You will already know some of this but a couple of points are worth re-stating. Don't let a stranger pat your puppy or dog on the head. They can bring their hand slowly towards them from the side so he can sniff the hand. If your puppy starts to back away this is a sign of fear and an early communication from your dog, so try to notice it and don't ignore it. If your puppy starts to yawn or lick his lips then this is the next level of communication, and he is really trying to tell you and the other person that he is uncomfortable. The final warning will be a bark. He will only get to this stage if nothing else has worked.

The best way to try and teach him that someone is not to be feared is to reward your puppy when he sees them so that it creates a positive association. You can also try showing your puppy that there is nothing to fear by touching, perhaps shaking a hand, and quietly talking, and while you are doing this reward your puppy with a high-value treat.

What not to do

If your dog does not return to you when you call him simply go and retrieve him and put him on his leash. Don't be angry with him just put him on the leash and move him away from whatever it is that is distracting him. This in itself, lets him know that coming back is a much better option.

Don't keep calling the same cue over and over again. For example, if he does not come when you call and you keep repeating the cue louder and louder the cue itself will lose its value and your puppy will simply tune it out as noise. If your cue isn't working then choose a new one and train your puppy to know what it is.

Don't have one person only training him if he lives with other family members. If your puppy is a family dog then everyone needs to be involved in the training and everyone needs to use the same cues. Ideally, everyone should be involved in the daily training, even for just a few minutes and everyone should proof before they go with him for a walk off-leash.

Never punish your puppy when he fails. This is particularly important with recall (and with separation anxiety). If you get angry with them or punish them when they finally return to you after not coming back right away all he will learn is that coming back to you is not a good experience and that it has negative consequences. It is not fun. All this will do is make his recall worse, not better.

Don't use the "come" cue if your dog is fully focused on something else and is unlikely to hear you. In this case, use his name to get his attention and to check that he can hear you (does he react by turning slightly towards you or twitch his ear). If he does, then use his "come" cue. If he is far away you can use a whistle or whistle yourself or use your hand signal.

Only use your "come" cue if you think it is likely to succeed. If you call and he does not come just walk over to him. Don't give him into trouble or reward him. If he does not 'come' then he is not fully trained, and you will want to re-start the training to the point he was succeeding, and build it up again from there.

Finally, do no use the recall cue for things they might not like doing. For example, don't associate it with a bath, or getting groomed, or having a tick removed. If you say the word bath to Millie she usually runs upstairs and hides which is why I have used bath as an example. Some dogs love a bath! The main point is that you need your puppy to associate your recall cue "come" with something he is going to like.

Games

You will use games for lots of reasons. One of the things you want to get your puppy to do is to watch you and know where you are. You always want to be moving around so that he knows he needs to keep an eye on you all the time.

Hide and go seek is also a great game to play. I love it more than the dogs and you probably will too.

This is a fun game that teaches them to pay attention to you. I still play hide and seek with them just to remind them to watch me and know where I am.

If you have forgotten how to play, hide behind a tree or a wall or any object. Let him run over to you and then come out, praise him and give him his treat.

A good way to play a game that reinforces paying attention to you (and can help remove any anxiety if other dogs are approaching) is to have them walk slightly in front of you and throw a really nice (and smelly) treat near you both for no apparent reason. This helps your puppy know that you might do something fun when he isn't expecting it.

A game I have found particularly good with my spaniels is ball play. They play with their ball all the time and always need to come back to have me throw it for them. It means when I am out with them, they rarely leave me. Barney, in particular, is obsessed with his ball - probably a bit too much.

Millie moves between balls, sticks and she loves pine cones (in the winter she loves to find a lost glove). They might surprise you with the things they love to retrieve (I call it 'fetch'). Frisbees are also popular and we had a retriever who loved a Frisbee.

Another great game is chase. As the name suggests, as your puppy is coming towards you give them lots of praise and get them to chase you. Some dogs love this game and others just don't have any interest in it so this will depend on your own puppy. But changing up the reward and keeping things exciting and different for your puppy is really important or they might get bored with you. Chase can also be done at any time.

Never play chase the other way around. Never chase your puppy or dog as a game. We see this a lot especially on TV because it is funny to watch but it really will mean your puppy just won't understand what you want. Chasing teaches him the opposite of what you want for recall and being able to take hold of him, especially if you need to do it quickly. It will be very confusing for him when he doesn't get rewarded with a game when he runs away from you. As cute as it can be, it can cause all sorts of problems.

Finally, and one last example of a fun game is piggy in the middle which everyone can join in. As the name suggests, someone calls your puppy's name and gives them a treat then someone else calls his name and he runs to them and gets a treat, and so on. This is actually great fun and a great way to get comfortable when you go to the park for the first time.

Your puppy will let you know what games and toys he likes best.

LEASH AND HEEL TRAINING

Leash training is a natural partner to recall training because many of the foundations are the same.

For example, your puppy will need to know his name and you will also need to train your puppy to look at you outlined in Chapter 1.

How to hold the leash

With your puppy on the left-hand side, hold the end of the leash in your right hand with the lead across the front of your body so that you are holding the other end of the leash in your left hand, with your hand closed over the leash, palm-side down. The treats will be in your right hand.

Ideally, start with your puppy in the sit position, and say 'let's go' or pat your side and start to walk. Control him with your left hand and say the cue 'close' or 'heel' while holding a treat in front of his nose just where you want him to be.

As you change direction use something to describe the change such as 'this way' or 'over here' - don't use over here is you are using the word 'here' as the cue call from 'come'.

To start this training, you can also simply put him on his leash and say nothing. It is likely that when you stand still there will be tension on the leash or you can create it by taking a step back or letting him take a step forward, which is more likely. Drop a treat beside your foot that is nearest to him and as soon as the tension releases, as he moves to get the treat, click if you are using a clicker. Just keep repeating as tension is created and released. This will help him understand that a loose leash brings better rewards.

Now that he can understand that you want a loose leash, then it is time to try walking. The only way to get a dog to stop pulling on a leash when you are walking is to teach the heel cue.

Walking to heel

Like recall, walking to heel on or off-leash is a part of daily life and therefore this training is vital. You will want to build it into his daily training routine and do it 2 or 3 times a day for 5-10 minutes.

Heelwork training is one of those times you want to make sure your puppy is hungry so that the treats can have maximum effect and reward. You might also find that you have to retrace the training slightly more often to ensure he is always successful.

Establish the heel position

The perfect heel position is to have your puppy's head or neck in line with the knee or leg. For ease, you can use his collar as a guide.

Like all of his training, you are going to show him what you want him to do and then you are going to teach him the word that describes what he is doing and that he wants to do it.

There are two ways you can do this that I have found work well and one shows on-leash and one shows off-leash.

1. Start with your puppy in front of you with the leash around your right-hand wrist while controlling the leash with your left hand. Place

your left hand about halfway down his leash towards his collar. Hold a treat in your right hand.

Get his attention by saying his name (or using a squeaky toy) and move your left leg back a step but remain stationary. Use the treat in your right hand to encourage him towards you and into the correct position and as you do this move your left leg back into position. You will encourage him to move in a semi-circle to get into the correct position. As soon as he is in the position you want to mark with a click and a treat. You can then add the signal (I use a point signal) by holding the treat in the same hand that I am using to point down by my side. Once he understands this signal add the verbal cue heel.

2. Start with your puppy in front of you with a treat in both hands. Hold out your hand and show him the treat in your right hand and then guide him around your back until he can see the other hand with a treat in it. In this example my left hand. It is this hand that will take him to the side of your leg and the final heel position. When he reaches the heel position praise him (or click) and give him his treat. Keep repeating until he understands the behavior.

Once you have done this a few times remove the treat from the hand that starts the movement (but keep doing the same routine) and keep the treat in the hand that guides him into the heel position. You will start to use the empty hand to create a visual cue such as pointing out to the side (you could even start by doing this before you remove the treat).

After he has got the hang of this you can start introducing your verbal cue of 'heel'. Say 'heel' point and he should move behind you into the heel position to get his reward.

Walking

One important tip with walking to heel is not to constantly hold the treat in front of your dog's nose. It will be tempting, but it won't teach him what you need him to learn.

To build movement into his heelwork and to starting walking, bring him to the heel position while stationary but don't give him the treat right away. Just bring him to heel, and then take a step forward so that he moves with you, and then reward him with his treat. Once he moves with you without hesitation move 2 steps and 3 steps and so on.

Don't forget to give him lots of encouragement which will also want to look at you. Every time he walks beside you in the correct position click and praise and reward, and slowly build more time and steps between the reward. You are aiming to have him happily walking beside you in a straight line with only praise and lots of encouragement.

Once he is walking in a straight line you can then get him used to a change of direction. You can start to do this in lots of different ways but you can start by simply turning left or right. Eventually, you will build in the other cues of 'this way' to change direction and his 'sit' cue. For example, you can ask him to sit after walking a few steps or before you change direction. Variations, as you move through his training, will keep him engaged especially as he starts to understand what you want him to do to get his reward.

Keep talking to your puppy and making lots of noises as you do this work - you want him to keep focused and interested in you. This will really help.

As you start walking with your puppy the leash should be relatively loose. If there is tension just stop and wait until when the leash slackens start to walk forward again. This will ensure that he can learn that there is only forward movement when the leash is slack. This works incredibly well and I still sometimes use it with Barney to this day.

Meeting other dogs while on the leash

When a dog is on a leash and he meets another dog the most likely meeting will be head-on and, as we already know, this behavior is rude in the world of dogs - and can even be seen as aggressive. Being on a leash, by the nature of the leash-itself, makes this kind of meeting more likely even if it is unintended by the dogs.

What you do to try to avoid encountering this behavior can unintentionally make things worse.

For example, if your dog is on a leash and he goes forward to another dog to say hello, and you pull him back and say 'no'.

1. This might start to create and build a negative association with other dogs.
2. If your puppy enthusiastically approaches another dog on the leash then this dog may not respond well even although they are normally friendly dogs. Again, his association with other dogs might be that they are hostile and he won't understand that it was triggered his over-enthusiastic approach. In this case, he might start building a defensive reaction to other dogs to look after himself.

How to greet other dogs on the leash

You need to train your puppy how to meet other dogs when they are on the leash and the best way to do this is to distract them from the other dog as they are approaching you both, and then to get him to greet the other dog without you or him making a fuss.

Start by training this with other dogs that he might know and then introduce dogs he doesn't know but that that you know are friendly.

To do this with dogs that are coming towards you, use distraction until the other dog is near or has passed by. Just make sure that you are the one that gets your puppy's attention.

You are trying to get him used to other dogs approaching while on his leash without building any negative associations and you are doing this by not allowing any situation to arise because he is focused on you and not an approaching dog.

You will approach it like this whether he is on or off-leash but when he is on the leash he is going to feel more constrained and he has fewer options in how he greets the oncoming dog.

The best way to do introduce your puppy to another dog while he is on the leash, and teaching him that he can do this as long as his leash is not being pulled, is to use direction change. As he starts to pull towards another dog change direction by saying your direction change cue, for example 'this way'. This also releases the tension on the leash. Remember to reward him. Keep moving in the direction of the other dog. If you are a sailor this might remind you of tacking. When you get there ask him for a sit. Once he is sitting you can talk to the other owner and he can sniff the other dog (just make sure you know this dog is ok with this) but try to use the cue 'go play' to let him know he can do this and to get him used to it.

CONCLUSION

Recall training encapsulates almost every element of training your puppy will need other than potty and crate training. As well as bringing in all the cues such as sit and stay and the recall cues of come and heel (for walking beside you) it keeps your puppy, and later your dog, safe.

Some of the training steps might take longer than others, but try to do them and complete them at the pace that works for your puppy. Just remember that our words mean nothing to a dog and we are teaching them both a word and an action that we want them to do.

Another aspect of this is not to give up. As you see your puppy progressing try not to settle for 'good enough'. I have done this too. Barney was 'good enough' and this was the case for his first few years, but as he got older, he became bolder and more confident and this is when I wished he knew his recall better, it wasn't until then that 'good enough' was just not good enough.

If you have 2 dogs then try to find the time to train the younger puppy away from the other dog. This was a mistake that I made and it is one I regret. I know it is very hard to find the time to take two dogs out separately and that a part of this is feeling guilty about leaving one behind, but it won't be forever. I ended up with one well trained dog (who had been my first dog, Millie) and one partially trained dog (the new puppy, Barney). I had to go back and train Barney again when he was older. He's a great dog, and did do lots of things right but, as I have described, his recall and leash training needed to be much better.

Finally, good recall means that you and your dog can spend many happy hours together in parks, on beaches, in forests, and hills and places you need to go. It means he can share as much of your life as he can and you are able to share, and you will never worry about him being safe. Just don't forget to always keep an eye out for him, sometimes he won't be aware of dangers that he can't know about or see and for recall to work we need to use it and to be able to use it when it matters most.

All dogs are different and some breeds will find different aspects of the training harder. If you are getting frustrated or stuck then take your dog to training classes or to a trainer. These training sessions can be invaluable and will sort out what you are doing wrong quickly.

CAN'T LIVE WITHOUT YOU? 1
IN 5 DOGS ARE LIKELY TO
SUFFER FROM SEPARATION
ANXIETY.

INTRODUCTION

Does your dog jump all over you when you return home or mess-up the house when you are out? Chew your furniture or your shoes? Do you hate leaving home because your dog looks so sad when you leave? Have your neighbors told you that your dog barks when you are not home? Do you feel guilty that you are a bad parent to your dog every day, every time you leave the house? Your dog may have separation anxiety. And you might have it too.

Separation Anxiety is now one of the biggest reasons that people give up their dogs for adoption and it is easy to understand why some owners feel they just have no options left.

It is very painful for us, the owners of our beautiful pups. We suffer with worry and guilt every day when we leave the house. But we also worry about the noise they make for our neighbors and of the mayhem we will face in the house when we get home.

Separation Anxiety can be helped and it can even go away altogether making your dog happy and making you love your dog all of the time. You can look forward to coming home knowing they too, had a good day without you. The sooner you start training your dog not to fear your departure the easier it will be and the faster you can feel good about yourself knowing that the dog you love so much is happy too.

Separation anxiety affects at least 1 in 7 dogs in the United States with some studies reporting it might be as high as 1 in 5. New Research from Finland has found that as many as 70% of our dogs are suffering from some kind of fear – and the most common is the fear of noise.

Anxiety can be a major source of stress and anxiety for you too. The constant barking or howling when you leave can be a source of aggravation for neighbors - this is a big problem. The behavior and destruction caused can also be a significant issue and the constant worry of leaving your pet means a living problem each and every day - and a constant source of worry and guilt.

The very best thing you can do, if you have a new puppy or a newly adopted dog, is to train your pup as soon as you can. Separation training is not generally top of the training list for new puppies - we all know sit, stay, leash and potty training and recall. But one of the most important training that needs to be done to make sure you have a happy life with your dog is making sure that you teach them that it is okay to be home alone.

Older dogs can, and do, develop separation anxiety too, and this can be for several different reasons and it has happened to my dogs.

I have 2 dogs and both experienced separation anxiety following the stay-at-home rules and work-from-home during the pandemic lockdown. The younger one had experienced separation anxiety at a younger age and it returned following the lockdown period. This book should help you to understand some of the basics of what can be done to help both you and your dog manage this fear.

In this book, I am going to explain to you how to help your dog if he or she has separation anxiety (and how you can tell if they do have separation anxiety), how to prevent separation anxiety if you have a new puppy so that he or she grows up happy to be left home alone when you need to go out to work, to school or need to go out for any other reason, or how to help an older or adopted dog with separation anxiety.

The remedies are easy when you know what they are and by the end of this book, you should know exactly what to do to help your puppy or dog be comfortable and relaxed when you need to leave them alone. By solving the problems with your four-legged family member it will mean you can leave home happy and in the knowledge that your dog is comfortable and relaxed while you are away - and returning home won't be too much of a surprise.

Separation anxiety in dogs is a common problem and is no fault of the owner. It is no fun for either the dog or the owner and so it's important to solve the problem.

The most common reason for anxiety in dogs is easy to deal with. We only need a little bit of patience, understanding, and love.

The results can be life-changing for both you and your dog and are simple to achieve with a little bit of patience and a few treats!

Some of the things you are going to learn about in this book include:

- What causes separation anxiety
- How to identify separation anxiety
- Preparing the room for separation
- Leaving and Returning
- Exercise, off Leash and Recall
- Games You Can Play

I have lived with dogs almost all of my life and during that time I have been involved in 3 litters being born (I was the mid-wife each time). Every dog is different and, even at a very young age, you can see the different personalities of a puppy.

Each puppy will stumble and walk or learn to eat solid food at a different pace from their siblings. This is true of training a dog too. They will all go at their own pace and respond to different techniques.

I currently have two beautiful Cocker Spaniels (mother and son) and for the first time, I had to deal with separation anxiety myself after the lockdown of 2020 and 2021. This was the first time that I had to train for separation anxiety in an older dog (or dogs that were not puppies).

Along the way, I noticed a few things that I had not been paying attention to. Today, I have two happy dogs, that don't mind me leaving the house. It has been a huge relief. It isn't difficult and you don't need any equipment - you only need to pay attention to what your dog is telling you and give them some time.

I hope you enjoy this book and that, by the end of it, you know what to do and how to help both your and your dog recover from separation anxiety.

What is dog training?

The dog training most commonly used and know is the type of dog training where a reward is provided for behavior required is known as associative learning or operant conditioning. The repeated application of a reward on the action will, over time, mean that the behavior is repeated. It is not only dogs that get trained in this way, humans do too as well as other animals.

It is used to change the conditioning of the dog to fit into the life of its owner - known also as the companion or the human-family.

Whenever and however you are training your dog, try to remember that your dog is also an individual animal with unique and special behavior. He communicates without speech which means we need to notice what signals our dog is giving us to attempt to communicate and let us know how he or she is feeling. In this sense, the dog is training us as well.

Take time to notice and watch your dog. He will be communicating with you all the time.

WHAT IS SEPARATION ANXIETY?

WHAT IS IT?

Separation Anxiety can be a form of separation distress or isolation distress - a milder form of separation anxiety. I use the terms separation anxiety as a general term but it will depend on the depth of the issue for your dog.

Separation anxiety happens when a dog reacts to separation (usually when their 'family' leaves the home) and this results in your dog getting stressed. This stress is released in a variety of ways, from whining and barking, to chewing and destruction with a few poops in between.

This book is not intended for those dogs with serious anxiety problems but rather a guide to help with some of the basic steps to ease your and your dog's anxiety with separation - and to also explain why they feel the way they do.

Dogs are used to living with others. They are pack animals, and in nature, are never alone. As mans best friend this means their pack includes us and everyone else we may live within our homes. In its simplest form, being 'separate' is not a natural experience for a dog.

Humans can, and do, live more separately. We are used to it because we need to do things like go to work, we might need to go to school or we just need to go shopping. We are therefore asking our dogs to behave unnaturally. This means that we need to teach them how to live in our world where some form of separation is a necessity.

Try to remember that for us our dogs, no matter how much we love them, are our pets. But, to them, we are a part of their pack. They see us as their family. They make no distinction between being human or not. And so it is natural for them to be with us and to follow us around - just like they would do with their pack.

One of the ways to think about this is to ask yourself this question:

How does your dog see you? If your dog thinks they are responsible for you, this might mean that they think of themselves as a kind of 'parent' and you are their child who they need to protect and look after.

Like parents of children, this means that they are going to get anxious when we leave and they will want to check up on you all the time to make sure we are safe and well. They will worry when they can't see you or know that you are safe.

Equally, if you think the dog feels more like the 'child' then they will fear their protector leaving them alone.

This was, and still is, spoken about in terms of who is dominant but it's more about who is the parent and who is the child in terms of any kind of hierarchy where it is a feeling of responsibility rather than power.

Your dog might feel that she is responsible for you and for keeping you safe and protected or she might be the child, seeking protection and safety. If you think about this and remember this, then understanding why your dog feels like they do, and why they behave in the way that they do, then it will start to make more sense and make it easier to stay calm when they misbehave.

There are a few theories on why dogs react the way that they do but the most important thing to know is that if they are suffering from any degree of separation anxiety then, for one reason or another, they are getting stressed when you leave and they are being left alone.

That is probably all that we need to acknowledge and then all we need to do is to help teach them that being alone without you is not to be feared.

Not all dogs are the same

Separation or canine separation anxiety can affect all dogs. Although research suggests that dogs are more likely to develop separation behavior problems if they are male, come from a shelter, or are separated from the litter before they are 60 days old. Interestingly dogs that were born at home were more likley to suffer anxiety than those born with a breeder (this might explain why Barney, who was born at home. Is more anxious than his mother, Millie).

Separation anxiety can and does, occur for other reasons. It affects puppy's, dogs beyond the puppy stage, or even more grown-up dogs.

Dogs that tend to have higher levels of alertness, which are more common in some types of breeds than others, are also thought to increase the chance of that dog experiencing separation anxiety. In research, mixed breed dogs were more likely to destroy, urinate or defecate when left alone, whereas Wheaten Terriers were likely to vocalize, salivate or pant.

It doesn't mean that all dogs of the same breed will develop separation anxiety, it just means that there is a higher tendency that they might be more susceptible.

And where separation anxiety existed, almost all of the dogs also had a fear of noise. Miniature Schnauzers and Staffordshire Bull Terriers were the least affected by noise.

It doesn't mean that all dogs of the same breed will develop separation anxiety, it just means that there is a higher tendency that they might be more susceptible.

Some examples of these breeds, in no particular order, are:

- Border Collies are not only highly alert but also very human-focused.
- German and Australian Shepherds due to their high levels of vigilance and loyalty.
- Bichon Frises and Chihuahuas as companion dogs who love sitting around on your lap or getting carried around in your purse. They are used to being with you all the time.
- Cocker Spaniels and King Charles Spaniels, just like the Labrador and Collie, Spaniels have been trained to work with us and strive to make us happy.

CAUSES AND SIGNS OF SEPARATION ANXIETY

WHAT CAUSES SEPARATION ANXIETY?

Separation anxiety is not a failure on the owner's part and there can be many reasons that a dog reacts like this.

There may have been a change in ownership either from another home or from a shelter, there may have been a house move or a change in the routine of the family, it might be due to divorce or the loss of a family member (usually another dog but it could be a cat or even a family member moving away to school).

For puppy's, it might simply be the first time they have been left alone having been used to being around people all the time.

Dogs may also have had a bad experience - firecrackers, a delivery person, or the noise from trash pick-up. Dogs don't like sudden and unexpected noises.

I know a dog that experienced the noise of a firecracker while in someone's garden (the firecracker was not close by) and the dog would shake and cower whenever it had to visit the home where it heard the noise for years later (it was a Cocker Spaniel).

Like anyone, dogs can get more nervous if they are alone. But remember dogs are not used to dealing with threats alone, they are used to packs who are there for safety as well as nurture.

If they are already nervous or uncomfortable then they will feel even more vulnerable when they need to deal with these 'threats' alone in their home.

Finally, dogs may be bored. Boredom usually affects young or energetic dogs who still don't know what to do when they are left to play - or relax - alone and they will seek out ways to keep themselves entertained. Like chewing furniture - this is also a calming activity - or exploring the trash. Exercise will help with this and this is covered later.

During 2020 and into 2021 dogs will have got used to their human family being around all the time - in my case my dogs did not even want to go out for a walk with their dog walker if I was staying in the house.

I resolved this by creating a home office and using that to work away from them but within easy reach, rather than working in the body of the house where they always were - and by doing more exercise with them and introducing new games.

In the example of the lockdown time, many dogs will have needed to learn how to separate all over again as people returned to work - just like they did when they first came to live with us.

This means that if you have needed to be at home for a longer time for any reason then your dog may need a reminder of how to deal with you not being there.

Signs of Separation Anxiety

Dogs will do some of these things some of the time. But when they display this behavior some or most of the time then it is likely your dog is suffering from some degree of separation anxiety.

Don't forget that dogs will get bored when they are left alone. Your dog will sleep – dogs sleep for between to 10 to 14 hours a day - but he will be awake at various points and he will be looking for something to do. He might have a stiff around, have a drink or two, and then look for something else to occupy his mind, his energy, and his time.

Dogs like to put things in their mouth, some things fit in their mouths and some things don't. This means that sometimes the mess you discover on returning home is simply a sign of a bored dog and not necessarily one suffering from anxiety.

This doesn't make the experience of returning home any more pleasant but exercise will help and finding toys that they can play with will relieve some of that boredom. Other signs, that are more likely to be separation anxiety, are more obvious.

The first thing I noticed was howling when I left the house. I didn't notice it - one of my neighbors told me that when the dog walker dropped them off after their walk they would howl for hours. Until this point, I had no idea.

This not only made me feel like a bad dog parent, but it also made me feel like a bad neighbor.

I would then leave the house for a few minutes and wait outside to see if this was an occasional thing or something they did all the time. Sure enough, after a few minutes, I would hear the howling.

This made it very hard for me to leave the house without worrying about them - and my neighbors. Commonly, the signs of distress manifest almost as soon as you leave the house.

Howling was not something I thought that they ever did. I didn't even know that they could do it. It only started to happen when the second puppy, Barney, got a bit older (the son of the older dog, Millie).

I initially thought that it might be that he began feeling anxious and spread this fear to his mum. She was always happy to be home alone.

I then thought back to how I had trained my first dog, who had been very happy being left for up to 4 hours, and started to work out the differences in how they had been both nurtured and trained.

Howling or barking is not the only sign of separation anxiety. Other signs are excessive barking, panting or whining, and indoor accidents. This won't be due to not being housebroken.

Stress can result in either peeing or pooping or both. They may also chew things to calm themselves, scratch at doors or windows and some might try to escape.

They are more likely to be scratching the door that you left from, or the window from where they can see you leave, they might chew something that smells of you - a shoe, sock, or even a magazine.

Signs of general stress in dogs will be panting and pacing and this may well be evident in your dog if he or she is suffering from separation anxiety.

Is your dog panting when you return home? This might be due to whining and barking while you were gone. You will notice this at other times too.

Separation Anxiety is not only when you leave the house and the dog is alone. It can also be when dogs become anxious when they are not seated near you or can't see you even if you are still at home.

Does your dog follow you around and want to sit beside you all the time. Do they sit against your legs or feet (this way they will know as soon as you move)?

What happens when you leave? Is it only you that your dog is focused on (if you share your home with family). In some cases, it doesn't matter if the dog is with another person in the home when you leave.

If you share your home and want to find this out, simply have a friend or another family member stay with your dog (with some treats) and leave the house. How does your dog react? Do they ignore the treats and look for you and if they do, how long for? Or do they settle down with the other person and enjoy their treats?

If you are not sure how your dog is reacting when you leave then it is useful to record your dog when you are not there. What does he do when you leave? Does he go to the door for a few minutes - how long? Take note of everything you can see and what he does. This is one of the best ways to find out what is happening when you are gone.

What to watch out for

Does your dog start to behave differently as you get ready to leave, either before you have started to get ready or when you are getting ready to leave? My dogs started to react to me picking up my coat or my car keys. If I was going on a trip - which might only be once every few months, one of my dogs would immediately start to pace around and look 'sad' as soon as I got a suitcase out.

And whenever I packed any kind of clothes into a bag she would try to get into the bag. If I was packing the same bag for a trip where they were also coming along on - they displayed different behavior.

They, and Millie, in particular, would be excited. Running around and trying to play as I packed. In the example of the coat, it could be that my coat also meant a walk and therefore they were excited for a walk rather than of separation. But the suitcase behavior was clearly not about being excited about a fun walk.

The first thing to do is to take notice of the behavior and any other behavior and try and think about if it has changed and why it might have changed. What changes have you made, if any?

Notice how much and how often your dog is following you (even if he is a new puppy). If it's an older dog try to think back to any changes - is he sitting beside you more often, following your more than he used to? Is there any other reason or a point in time that you can identify?

The solution to this part of their behavior is to slowly build them up to being comfortable with you not being beside or near them so that they get used to your absence and learn (or re-learn) that you come back. In my early days of re-training Barney, that was one thing that made me feel better - that he knew I would come back and would learn that I came back. Of course, there is much more to it than this but it made me feel better at the time.

You also need to teach your dog not to follow you around the house all the time and you will need to get them to go to different places or rooms in the house without you by their side or in view.

Other signs of a nervous or anxious dog or puppy

- Cowering - this is usually caused by fear (which causes a different type of stress)
- Shaking - this is commonly a sign of nervousness or the dog feeling uncomfortable - it is caused by their raised levels of adrenalin
- Abnormal behavior - are they showing any unusual behaviors like not playing the way they would normally (not fetching the ball, etc)

It is perfectly natural for dogs to show some anxiety - so don't over-react or worry about it. But if they do suffer from anxiety or nervousness, it is more likely they will also suffer from separation anxiety. This is the category that Barney fell into.

Sometimes any or some of the signs can be there for other reasons so if you are worried at all just check with your veterinary.

WHY PUNISHMENT WON'T WORK

Before we talk about all the things that can be done to help with separation anxiety it is useful to understand why punishment just won't work.

Have you ever taken your dog over to the 'scene of the crime' and pointed at it. I have done this and we all will have done this.

Notice that the dog appears to look guilty and might cower. We, as humans, project our feelings or interpretation onto this behavior and assume that the dog is noticing what it has done and feels 'guilty' about it.

This is not what is happening. What we see as 'looking guilty' is appeasement behavior. It can be a way that your dog is releasing tension to try and get rid of their fear. The cowering, flat ears and tail between the legs or looking away is your dog trying to placate you.

The dog will know that she emptied the trash all over the kitchen floor and dragged some of it into other rooms but it won't connect what it has done wrong.

And if definitely won't connect something that happened 2 or 3 hours ago to anything by the time you arrive home to find the mess.

All your dog will know is that you are not happy and it will pick this up and be fearful and will try to placate you but it won't know what it has done, it only knows you are unhappy right now - no matter how much you point at that mess your dog is not going know why you are angry.

Dogs won't associate something done hours or even minutes ago with the here-and-now. No matter how much we tell them, they simply won't understand why we are angry with them - just that we are.

And this means they won't understand why they are being punished. They will only connect that you arrive home and they get punished.

This all means that punishment when you return home will make the dog not only stressed about you leaving but stressed about you coming home too. This can make any anxiety worse.

Just remember, the dog has not done this to deliberately annoy you nor to 'get back' at you. Dogs just don't think like that. They did it because they were stressed and anxious and they tried to use that pent-up energy.

They might look 'guilty' when you return because they have learned that they got into trouble the last time you came back - so they appease you as soon as you return.

But they are doing this because when you return, they sometimes get punished, so they react to prevent it as much as they can.

PREPARATION AND SOCIALIZATION

PUPPY'S

You might not realize this, but puppy socialization during its first 3 to 5 months is very important for your dog's mental health as it grows up.

Try not to overlook this aspect of your puppy's training. We went to the local veterinary as soon as our first puppy, Millie, arrived.

It simply involved being with 6 or 7 other puppies in the reception areas all playing together or having a bark at each other. The owners were also important for the puppies as they got to meet other adults or children who were not family members to our puppy.

It's a simple thing to do but so important and much more important than I had realized at the time.

The dogs learn boundaries, how hard to bite (or not to bite), and how to play with other dogs. Dogs communicate with each other all the time and this early socialization helps them understand this.

Because Barney had been born at home, I knew how he played with his other siblings and he had other dogs he knew around him (as well as his mother, his dad, his aunty, and his grandma !). I didn't take him to these puppy socialization classes. He did go to the puppy training classes like his mum, but he missed out on these early socialization classes.

Try not to overlook how important the first weeks and months are for a puppy and how it can affect them later. Research has shown that the experiences a puppy has at this time can have a profound effect on their behavior in the future and their levels of anxiety.

Preparation for separation

In terms of preventing separation anxiety, it's a good idea to get your puppy used to being separated from you when they are young. Even if you don't expect to be away from them there will be times when you will need to.

Teaching your puppy not to fear this absence and to let them know that they can be relaxed when you are not there is one of the best things you can do for both your puppy and for yourself.

If your puppy can get used to being left for short periods when they are young then they are more likely to grow up feeling relaxed and comfortable when left on their own for part of the day.

These are all really simple things to do and are obvious once you know them. You will need to do this slowly and teaching them bit by bit over time.

The first 3 basic steps you need to take are the following ones.

Decide on your puppy or dogs room

1.Pick the room you want your puppy or dog to be in when you are not in the house - either in their basket, bed, or crate. Decide which room this is going to be as early as you can. I did this with Millie but not with Barney. They were both able to come to work with me when he was young so I didn't consider this as well as I did with Millie. It meant he missed out on this training too, as a younger puppy. On reflection, he didn't have have his own place in the room.

2.Once you decide on where this is, start getting them used to being in this room - don't wait until the time when you are going to leave the house. I never left them in another room. I had the crate in this room (doors open) and a basket.

3.Spend time with your puppy or dog in this room - you want them to understand it is not a punishment 'place' or a place that is apart from you but a part of their household.

The biggest mistake I made with Barney was number 1 from that list. I didn't provide his own or favorite place to settle in the room (he had Millie's basked to share). He did not have his own place. I also removed the crate as it was taking up so much space. This was a mistake. I had not realized that it was important to him - he knew it as his bed. Whereas I saw it as a cage, it was his 'safe place'. Worse, when I thought back, I realized that I also had a carry bag that he would use - I had also cleared that away at some point. The first thing I did was get one - and re-install a place for just Barney.

TRAINING FOR A HAPPY DOG
AT HOME

PREPARATION FOR DEPARTURE

Create a physical barrier between the room you want them to remain in and the room you are in - make this something they can see you through (like a gate).

Once you have picked the room that you want your dog to stay in when you leave the house, create a gate to the room but make it a barrier or gate so that your dog can still see you. Remember not to interact with your puppy or dog when they are in this room - just go about doing things as normal.

Don't forget to spend time with them in this room when you are not about to leave, spend time there during the day or when you are training them so that this becomes a place that you are a part of too.

As you begin their training, the first thing you will do after you have created the gate is to just be on the other side of the gate to your dog. Do this for 2 or 3 minutes but if your dog starts to get stressed just calmly let them out.

Keep building their confidence and slowly make the time longer. Start moving around and doing other things as you build up the time and distance. At this point, you will always be in sight.

If they start to get anxious just move forward or return to the point where they were comfortable. Once they are comfortable with the distance, start to move out of sight to another room for a few minutes and then repeat the process of stretching the time. Begin by moving to the door of the room.

Then move into another room out of sight (but they will still be able to hear and smell you). Return after a few minutes, and then repeat building up the time as you go along.

Finally, go to the main door and go outside for a few minutes. Once again repeat the process of increasing the time you are away and check how your dog is reacting. If there are signs of stress or anxiety just go back a couple of steps and begin building up your dog's confidence once again. Keep the time as short as you need to, it can start with as little as 5 or 10 seconds and build the time based on your dog's response.

Put their bedding or basket in this room along with any of their toys.

From the very start let the dog know that the place you have chosen is their safe place. Keep all their things in this room and place their bed or crate in here as soon as you can. If you using a crate, keep the crate door open - let them get used to going in and out of the crate and choosing to do so. Don't forget to spend time with them in this room.

Get some chew toys for them. Chew toys are good because chewing is calming action (and it's why they chew things they shouldn't). You could also put an item of your clothing in the room so that they can more easily smell you and feel more secure.

The chew toys help your dog use their mind to try and work out how to get the food or treat removed. Giving a reason for dogs to exercise their mind keeps them busy and happily occupied. A Kong is a great chew toy to use because, as well as the chewing, the fun of getting the treats or food out of the inside of the King exercises their mind.

There are some suggested toys at the end of the book along with some suggested games for more general playing.

Put on some sound - like a radio talk station. Not at a high volume - you only want to muffle any unexpected sounds.

This helps my dogs. I use either the television news or channel that is not likely to have shows with sudden noise but a talk radio station is probably better. Whatever you choose make it something that you listen to so that they are familiar with it.

Your dog will be paying attention to any noise they hear so this can help disguise some of the day-to-day noises that might go on outside (or inside) your home. It is useful to do this as soon as you begin the training so that it becomes familiar.

Teach your dog not to follow you all the time in the home

Try to teach your dog not to follow you all the time in the home and get them to go to different places in the house. Test them being in a room while you are in another. Don't force this or make them feel stressed about it. You need to teach them to be comfortable with it.

Play a game where you ask them to remain in one room while you move to another, then come back. If they stay where they were, come back and give them a reward - it can be a treat or affection/well done. Once again, do this calmly because if you do, then you will keep your dog calm too.

Remember when you come back not to increase or cause excitement. This can be a great game for your dog and they will enjoy it as much as you enjoy the results of it.

When you are ready to start the next phase of actually leaving the house there a few more things you can do to keep your dog calm while you are out.

One of the most important is exercise and this is explained in a later chapter.

Preparation summary

Do steps 1-3 together at the start and for short periods at first and, in the beginning, stay within their sights. Perhaps give them a chew toy and open the gate before they are finished chewing (stuffing a Kong with treats or food is a great way to do this). Just open the gate or remove the blocker and let them decide to stay in the room and finish chewing if they want to or let them leave if that's what they prefer.

Remember, you are trying to get your dog or puppy to be comfortable in their room or space. As they get more comfortable, start to move further away and eventually into another room where they can't see you (but can still hear you). Only start moving further away when you notice they are comfortable - and build them up to 30 minutes. This might take a few days.

HOW TO LEAVE AND RETURN

When you leave - don't get them excited. For example, don't say to them in a cute sad voice, "I won't be long! I'll be back soon!".

As you get ready to leave try and notice what they are reacting to as you get ready. For example, one of my dogs would start jumping around as soon as I got my boots out. Initially, I put them on in another room, and then I realized I had to be in control of their reaction. I put the boots on then didn't leave (you can do this with keys/coats etc, pick them up or put it on and just sit for a while).

You can also try body-blocking. I used this with the younger dog (he was more excitable). As soon as he started to get agitated as the boots or coat came out I interrupted his behavior by standing up straight and then asking him to go to his basket. It's important not to be angry

- they aren't doing anything wrong - you just want them to do something else so let them know what that is e.g. go to their crate or their basket.

Remember not to shout - dogs hear this as barking. And they can also pick up on the aggression of it (a shout can be heard as aggression). Their excitement means their adrenalin is pumping so you need to calm this down not increase it by making them feel fear on top of their separation anxiety.

Take this slowly - leave and come back. Build their knowledge. Having them exercised will help reduce their energy levels so remember to make sure they have had a walk and have been fed. This will make them tired. (Don't forget to leave water out for them).

You can also try giving them a favorite treat. This might help them associate your departure with something they can look forward to. Someone I know uses a hollowed-out bone with frozen dog food inside (they put the dog food in the bone then freeze it). You could do the same with a Kong.

If you have to go out to work - try not to be away for more than 2-3 hours at the start, eventually, 4 hours would be the ideal limit. If you need to leave them for the full day, get someone to come and visit them after 4 hours if you can or for a period of time, or try and dog walker as often as you can.

Remember dogs will pick up your anxiety about their anxiety! So try to be calm when you leave and when you return. .

When you return, don't get them excited with happy cries of "Hello!". Don't over-excite them or over-reward them when you come back. Just arrive home and then ignore them for 5 minutes. You need to make the exit and return a very normal thing rather than any kind of event to be excited about.

If they have done something wrong on your return don't punish them or shout at them. They won't understand why.

Summary

- Don't make a fuss of your dog when you leave. Don't and kiss them and say 'goodbye'.
- Leave calmly and without a fuss.
- Give them their favorite treat as you leave - give them something to chew on.
- Make sure they have been exercised.
- Don't excite them as soon as you return home, wait a few minutes before greeting them.

(These steps were the single most effective thing that I did to help my dog with separation).

LEAVING WHEN USING A CRATE

When you put your dog in their crate (if you use a crate) before you leave then don't close the door right away. Put them in and wait until they calm down or lie down.

This might take a few minutes or more so do something else and give them time to relax and be calm. Close and open the door a few times if you like but wait until they lie down before you close the door.

Don't bride them into the crate with a treat and then immediately shut the door - just take your time and let them take their time to get comfortable.

In terms of new puppies, puppies will get anxious when you leave them at night in the beginning. Don't forget this will be the first time they have not been with their mother or other members of their litter.

It will be their first experience of being alone. If you are using a crate make sure it is in the same room as you are in and get them used to it during the day when you are around. If you are using another room like a utility room then spend time in that room with them during the day and try to get them to go into it - add a toy or a chew.

Once they are comfortable in their space and their room then you can start moving away using the methods detailed in the first step.

Leave and return summary

Start by leaving the house for a minute, 2 minutes, 3 minutes, and so on and try and return before they are anxious. If you can, then leave for longer and build up to an hour and so on. If you notice they are not comfortable, then go back to the point when they were, and start from there again. Build the time up again. Aim to build the routine - perhaps a treat as you leave. But don't kiss and cuddle them and make a fuss with gestures and by your comments. Try and make it as normal and calm as possible.

Of everything I did to help with Barney's separation anxiety, this was single and most effective technique. It seems so simple yet it seemed to (and still does) calm him. I stopped saying goodbye or paying attention when I left. I just put on my coat. Made no fuss at all, and left calmly (not rushing).

Once you start leaving altogether, do for short periods at the start if you can, and build up the time to 2,3 and 4 hours. Do everything as normal and as they are now used to - and make sure they have something to play with or to eat.

Ideally, don't leave your dog alone for more than 4 hours. If you can ask a neighbor or a friend to visit - one your dog might know - or a dog walker. If you are able, come home from work for lunch.

You might start to notice that your dog starts to get anxious when you put on your shoes or coat or if you pick up keys or a bag.

If they start to react to these signs then start training them to get used to these things. Put on your shoes or coat or grab your keys but don't leave. Do something else or sit down and relax (or watch the TV). Keep doing this during the day so that they don't associate these things with your departure.

You might need to re-trace your steps a few times and go back a few paces in the separation training from time-to-time as you are building their confidence and their sense of 'normal'. Just go back to the point where your dog was last comfortable.

Exercise is an important part of curing separation anxiety and the reason for this are explained next.

EXERCISE, LEASH, RECALL AND GAMES

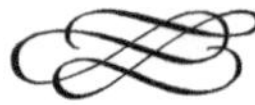

EXERCISE

If you leaving for a few hours then make sure they have been well excised before you leave.

A 2015 study by PLoS One found that dogs with noise sensitivity and separation anxiety had less daily exercise.

This suggests that exercise is one of the biggest things you can do (other than these things described in the previous chapters) to improve separation anxiety in your dog.

You need to make sure your pet gets lots of exercise every day because a tired, happy dog will be less stressed when you leave.

When they are younger shorter walks more often are better for them. 20 minute's walk, 4 times a day is enough. As they get older you will do longer walks less often. Always engage with your dog when you are taking them for a walk and try to play with them.

But it is also important to let your dog explore its mental agility too and let them play mental exercises as well as purely physical ones. I sometimes throw a ball in the opposite direction they are expecting and this is even better if they haven't noticed exactly where you have thrown it. Then we play a find the ball/fetch game.

It's important to engage with your dog during your walk and to play with them. Dog walking time isn't really about humans meeting up with each other in the park. It's our time to focus on the dog and to be fully with them. Stopping to talk is ok but not for the entire time that you are out with your dog.

Some dogs love going out to play with other dogs, some dogs like to play only with their owner and are not bothered by other dogs.

While there are traits across breeds you will still find that even within the same breed you will get both types of behavior.

I have Spaniels and I know quite a few and they are happy just to play with me and rarely with other dogs. Of the other dogs I meet regularly, I know a Cockapoo and they love to play with other dogs and try and get chased by them. Labradors like to play with others whilst Retrievers and German Shepards are less likely. Schnauzers like to have a good bark or shout at other dogs and some like to play with them too, but not all - a shout is enough fun.

But this isn't true of all of these breeds of dogs - some will behave like this whilst others won't.

This book isn't about the behavior of breeds or the differences between breeds but there are common traits within different breeds of dog. The comments I have made here are very general but I just wanted to point out that some dogs will simply just behave differently.

Dogs love to play and explore and they are fast learners. They actually like training. So play training games like fetch - a ball, frisby or stick.

Play games that they have to work out with their mind as often as you can. All games will help with separation anxiety because they will be tired.

You can get them to run around you as you hold a treat in your end then throw the treat forward and away from you. As they retrieve the treat have another one ready as they come back to you and repeat the game of going in a circle, holding out the treat so that your dog runs around you in a circle following your outstretched arm before throwing the treat forward.

This game helps with recall and makes coming back to you fun.

Another great game to play outside is hide-and-seek. This helps them make sure they pay attention to where you are! I hide behind a tree or a bush or sometimes just behind a wall.

By working their mind as well as their body they will be too tired to be anxious while you're gone. There are a few examples of the games you can play at the end of this book.

LEASH AND OFF-LEASH IMPACT ON EXERCISE AND ANXIETY

The 2015 PLoS One study found that dogs that were exercised off-leash were less likely to suffer from separation anxiety or fear around noise. The likely reason for this is that being on a leash, partly on a leash, or running free has an impact on the amount of exercise a dog has.

Leash training and recall are also not the subjects of this book and therefore I will only touch on the basics here but it is important in terms of getting your dog to behave off-leash so that they can be exercised more fully. Clicker training can also be used for leash and recall training where the reward is immediately preceded by the click. I have trained with and without the clicker.

There are lots of ways to train your dog both leash training and recall but these are two methods I have used that were quick, easy, and successful.

Leash training tips

If you have a new puppy, then start by letting the puppy run around with the lead on inside the house. Call them to you, pick up the lead for a few minutes and give your puppy a tasty reward.

Once you leave the house always carry small treats with you as you will need a lot of these during your puppy training process. I still use lots of treats when training dogs of any age.

Now you need to train yourself on how to hold the leash. Hold the handle of the leash in your right hand and then across the front of your body to the palm of the left hand (facing down) so that the left hand can gently control the length of the leash by simply moving it backward and forwards like a lever. You can use any hand that you and your dog are comfortable with as the anchor hand.

Walk with your dog beside you and hold a treat in your hand. Bring it over to the front of your dog's nose so he knows it's there. Every few steps say good boy and give him a small treat. Keep doing this eventually turning and walking in another direction with the dog beside you. Repeat the process of turning a walking a few steps. Reward and praise your dog often.

Build up this exercise and start moving around objects with your dog beside you on the leash - and start to let go of the leash, slowly releasing it so that it hangs loose. Then eventually let the leash go but keeping them beside you with the ever-present treat just held in your hand near their nose.

If your puppy (and this works for older dogs too) starts to pull, just stop walking and stand still. Call the dog to you and give them a treat. Once they relax the pressure, start walking again. It might take longer to get to the park but they want to get there too! This start-stop training really does work.

If your puppy sits down and refuses to move (or lays down in my case) then just walk a few steps away and call her and offer a treat. Again, just keep repeating every time they stop and sit or lay down, refusing to move.

RECALL TRAINING TIPS

Ask your dog to wait or stay - whatever you prefer. Get your dog to sit, then hold up your hand with the palm flat and tell your dog to wait (much like a traffic officer will do to stop the traffic). Slowly walk backward a few steps facing your puppy. Just go a few steps.

If they stay for just a few seconds ask them to 'come', say good boy and give them a treat. Keep repeating and increasing the stay time and the distance. Make it fun to come back to you so that coming back is a great experience.

You are teaching them what you want them to do and rewarding them so that they know they did what you wanted them to do and that you are happy with them (which is their main aim in life, to make you happy). Eventually, walk away with your back to them. As always, start with short distances and gradually build up to longer distances.

Always ask them to sit or wait in the same way - using hand signals is good as dogs are good at understanding these. Always ask them to 'come' or 'come here' or 'here' using the same words and the word that you prefer.

If you have a new puppy, it is really scary to let them off the leash for the first time. A game that works well is to go to the park with 2 people and your puppy. Basically, you play a game of puppy-in-the-middle. Each one calls to the puppy and when she comes, she gets a treat and lots of praise (or a ball). Then the other one calls and does the same thing so that the puppy is running to a different person each time. Remember to use the same call ('come here', 'here, or 'come' and the same hand signal). Using two people when you first let your puppy off-leash also means that you will be more relaxed because there are now two of you to help.

Some other useful tips

A dog whines when it starts to get tense or excited - think of as them releasing their energy. Sometimes they whine because they want something - if this is the case, they will make it obvious what they want. If you notice this and the reason is not obvious then try and work out why it might be excited and calm them down before the excitement level rises.

If you have multiple household members - try and share the dog equally amongst everyone - so the dog doesn't focus all their attention onto one person. If there are more members then one can leave and he dog will worry less. Research shows that dogs in multiple person households are more likely to suffer from separation anxiety – I had expected it to be the other way around.

Try and give the dog something new to learn each week or each day - a new game or mental exercise. Dogs love being challenged and it helps to ease their boredom. I play "find the cheese" - and hide bits of cheese around a room that they then need to find. They love this game.

4 Must Do's When Leaving

For me, it was the simple things that worked best with Barney.

There is no effusive goodbye when I leave them and I do my best to show no guilt when I depart. I just make sure that they both have water, that their toys are available or one of my socks that they like, and then I leave.

I now always walk them before leaving. By the time I leave both Millie and Barney are usually sleeping.

When I come back, for a few minutes I make no fuss at all. I don't normally manage 5 minutes but I wait as long as I can. I am, after all, just as happy to see both Millie and Barney as they are to see me.

Following and during lockdown, I created a room to work with no basket or chair for either of them - but mainly Barney. I leave the door open so they can come and go if they want. Right now Barney is sleeping by himself in the other room and Millie has just popped through for a visit.

Although the training in this book has helped my dogs, especially Barney, it won't help every dog and every owner. Separation is stressful for the owners as much as the dogs and finding a method of helping is something I will continue to work on and explore.

CONCLUSION AND SUMMARY

There is often never just one reason that your dog can become anxious or suffer from some form of separation anxiety. In Barney's case, there were lot of small things – no 'place' of his own, a big welcome when I came home, no puppy socialization classes and being born at home – any one of these, or just one could have made him more anxious. What was interesting is how many, apparent small things, there were.

When I addressed them all (or the ones that I could) he became much happier being left at home – and I do think the biggest was leaving without a big goodbye.

Just try and think about, and notice, the things that you do – you can be sure that your dog will notice all of them.

The Room

Pick the room you want your puppy or dog to be in when you are not in the house

Start getting them used to being in this room

Spend time with your puppy or dog in this room

THE 10 STEPS TO HELP SEPARATION ANXIETY

Preparation

1. Create a physical barrier between the room you want them to remain in and the room you are in - make this something they can see you through.
2. Put their bedding or basket in this room along with any of their toys and the bowls.
3. Put on some sound - like a radio talk station. Not at a high volume - you only want to muffle any unexpected sounds.
4. Teach your dog not to follow you all the time in the home.
Leaving & Returning
5. Don't make a fuss of your dog when you leave. Don't and kiss them and say 'goodbye'
6. Leave calmly and without a fuss
7. Give them their favorite treat as you leave - give them something to chew on
8. Make sure they have been exercised
9. When you return don't over-excite your dog as soon as you arrive home (if there is a mess, don't punish your dog)

10. Wait a few minutes before you acknowledge them and say
    hello.

GAMES

Here are a couple of simple games you can play with your dog.

Find The Cheese

My dogs just love this game. It also helps that they love cheese. But you can use any favorite treat. It's great for nose work too. I mix it up with a bit of sit and stay training (and being apart from me). Take them to the other side of the door of the room you are going to hide the cheese in. Ask them to sit they stay (I let them sniff the cheese in my hand). I give them a treat at this point.

Close the door - if they move as you do this just ask them to sit and stay until they do sit and stay.

Once they are doing sit and stay, close the door and go and hide the cheese. Open the door and tell them to 'Find The Cheese'. It is the funniest game to play and you might find yourself getting quite proud of clever hiding places.

Tug

Millie loves to play tug. I always let her win and it's great fun watching her face each time. I use an old rag or a toy with a soft part with a ball at the end but ropes with knots are common tug toys.

Hide something under a cup

3 cups, hide a treat under one, and move it around. Get your dog to sit and stay while you move the cups around and then ask them to find the treat.

Fetch

Fetch a ball or frisbee, really fetch anything. They will let you know what they prefer themselves and they might not even like a fetch game. I love this game more than my dogs and they love to fetch tennis balls (you can buy them in bulk second-hand on eBay for $20-$30).

It's always great when they bring something back to you and drop it at your feet and they love seeing me so delighted with them. Which I am.

Circle and Throw

Hold a treat in your hand and as you do hold out your arm and start to spin in a circle, holding out the treat so that your dog can smell it and so that he runs around you in a circle following your outstretched arm with the treat. Then throw the treat forward to let him fetch. Have another treat ready and repeat.

Ice Cubes

Believe it or not some dogs love playing with ice cubes! Try it out on your dog to see if he or she likes playing with them.

Toys

Kong - this is a favorite of most dogs. They come in all sizes and are great for stuffing treats or food or frozen food like soup or mince inside the Kong. Dogs love this game and enjoy trying to get the food out. It's also great fun to watch.

Any type of ball (some dogs prefer squeaky balls whilst others can become over-attached so work out which type your dog prefers). I have found the best balls are plastic ones that bounce a bit more than tennis balls, but again, you will be able to work out which type of ball your dog prefers. It's also useful to know that not all dogs like playing with balls.